PERIPLUS

Pocket JAPANESE Dictionary

Compiled by
Yuki Shimada

PERIPLUS

Published by Periplus Editions (HK) Ltd.

ISBN: 0-7946-0048-4

Printed in Singapore

Distributed by:

Asia-Pacific
Berkeley Books Pte Ltd
130 Joo Seng Road, 06-01/03
Singapore 368357
Tel: (65) 6280 1330
Fax: (65) 6280 6290
E-mail: inquiries@periplus.com.sg

Japan & Korea
Tuttle Publishing
Yaekari Building 3F
5-4-12 Osaki, Shinagawa-ku
Tokyo 1410032
Japan
Tel: (03) 5437 0171
Fax: (03) 5437 0755
E-mail: tuttle-sales@gol.com

North America
Tuttle Publishing
Airport Industrial Park
364 Innovation Drive
North Clarendon, VT 05759-9436
USA
Tel: (802) 773 8930
Fax: (802) 773 6993
E-mail: info@tuttlepublishing.com

Indonesia
PT Java Books Indonesia
Jl. Kelapa Gading Kirana
Blok A14 No. 17
Jakarta 14240
Indonesia
Tel: (62-21) 451 5351
Fax: (62-21) 453 4987
E-mail: cs@javabooks.co.id

Contents

Introduction	iv
Pronunciation	vi
Japanese–English Dictionary	1
English–Japanese Dictionary	43

Introduction

This Pocket Dictionary is an indispensable companion for visitors to Japan and for anyone in the early stages of learning Japanese. It contains all the 3,000 or so Japanese words that are most commonly encountered in colloquial, everyday speech.

For the sake of clarity, only the common Japanese equivalents for each English word have been given. When an English word has more than one possible meaning, with different Japanese equivalents, each meaning is listed separately, with a clear explanatory gloss. The layout is clear and accessible, with none of the abbreviations and dense nests of entries typical of many small dictionaries.

The language of this dictionary is that spoken universally throughout the islands of Japan, by some 120 million people. Japanese is not clearly related to any other languages of the world. There was no written form of Japanese until the early centuries CE, when the system that had long been in use in China was borrowed and adapted.

Written Chinese does not relate directly to the sounds of the language; instead it makes use of a very large number of characters representing different syllables, to each of which is linked both a meaning and a sound. The characters derived initially from the stylized representation of concrete objects, to which the abstract meanings needed for the expression of the complete language were added by processes of combination and metaphor.

The pronunciation of each of these characters is not obvious from the written form but must be learnt separately in each case. To make matters more complex, in Japanese each character (kanji) is usually associated with several possible pronunciations. One or more (the on readings) are derived from the Chinese syllable originally represented by the character, and others (the kun readings) from native Japanese elements of equivalent or associated meaning. Each reading is used in different contexts (for example when used alone or in compound words, as part of the general vocabulary or in proper names) and the choice is only partly predictable.

The Chinese language does not make use of inflections (changes to the form of a word to indicate grammatical information such as tense or number), so it can be effectively written in characters representing unvarying syllables. By contrast Japanese has many inflections, and the variable word endings and particles need to be represented in writing to prevent ambiguity. To this end a set of syllabic symbols (kana 'borrowed names'), derived from Chinese characters but with only sound values and no meaning component, are used in conjunction with kanji.

Thus in written Japanese the roots of words are represented by kanji, with the inflections and particles being in hiragana ('rounded kana'), derived from simplified cursive forms of certain kanji. Small versions of hiragana, known as furigana ('applied kana'), are also sometimes written above kanji to show their readings, for example in material for children or foreigners, or in case of ambiguity or some obscure characters used in personal names.

A second version of the same set of syllables, with more angular forms and known as katakana ('side kana', being derived from a part only of certain kanji) is also used for purposes such as transcribing foreign words and names, for representations of natural sounds, and sometimes for emphasis.

In this dictionary every Japanese word and phrase is also clearly spelled out in the roman alphabet (romaji).

In contrast with the complexity of the writing system, the pronunciation of Japanese is quite straightforward for English speakers: it is not a tonal language and syllables are evenly stressed. Distinguishing clearly between long and short vowels is important, as in several cases a completely different meaning can result. Long vowels are pronounced with twice the length of short vowels, effectively creating an extra syllable. In this dictionary they are indicated by a bar over the vowel concerned; elsewhere you may find them written with a double vowel, or with long e represented as ei and long o as ou, but these practices can be misleading to English speakers.

The Japanese-English section of the dictionary is alphabetized according to the romanised forms, with short vowels preceding the equivalent long vowels.

Pronunciation

Japanese is made up of strings of syllables (*a, ka, ta*, etc.) which join together following simple rules of pronunciation (e.g. *anata* is *a-na-ta*). Unlike English, each syllable has mostly even stress and combinations of vowels (*e-i, a-i*, etc.) do not represent completely new sounds.

Vowels

Japanese has five vowels, pronounced either long or short. Distinguishing the length is very important as sometimes the meaning depends on the difference (e.g. *ojisan/ojîsan*, terms of address to a middle-aged man and an old man respectively). Note that a final *e* is always pronounced.

a	like *a* in ***A**merica*	***a**sa*
â	like *ah* in ***ah**!*	*m**â***
e	like *e* in *p**e**t*	*d**e**su, sak**e***
ê	like *ere* in *th**ere***	***ê**tone*
i	like *i* in *p**i**t*	*n**i**ch**i***
î	like *ee* in *k**ee**p*	***î**e*
o	like *o* in *t**o**p*	*y**o**ru*
ô	like *aw* in *l**aw***	*ky**ô***
u	like *u* in *p**u**t*	*har**u***
û	like *oo* in *c**oo**p*	*ch**û***

Vowel combinations

Basically, each vowel should be pronounced separately. The most common combinations are:

ai	like *igh* in *h**igh***	*h**ai***
ao	like *ao* in the British pronunciation of *L**ao**s*	*n**ao***
ei	like *ay* in *pl**ay***	*r**ei***
ue	like *ue* in *p**ue**blo*	***ue***

Consonants

Most consonants are pronounced in a similar manner to English. Some that are a bit different are:

f	in native words, *fu* is like *foo* in ***foo**d*, but without pressing the teeth against the lips	***fu**yu*
	in loanwords, like *f* in ***f**inger*	***f**endâ*
n	at the end of a word, may be more like *ng* in *thi**ng***	*ye**n***
r	like *tt* in the American pronunciation of *bu**tt**er*	*a**r**e*

(You can use *l* for *r* at the beginning of a word and after *n*.)

Note: when *i* and *u* follow *k, s, t, p, h* or come between two of them, they become very shortened and are often not heard at all (e.g. *desu* becomes *des* and *mimashita* becomes *mimashta*).

Japanese—English

A

abura 油 oil
aburareta あぶられた roasted, grilled, toasted
aburu あぶる to roast, to grill
achiragawa あちら側 over there
agerukoto 上げること raise, lift
ago あご chin, jaw
agohige あごひげ beard
ahiru アヒル duck
ai 愛 love
aigandôbutsu 愛玩動物 pet animal
aijô 愛情 affection
aimai na あいまいな vague
airon o kakeru アイロンをかける（服の） to iron (clothing)
airurando アイルランド Ireland
airurando(jin) no アイルランド（人）の Irish
aisatsu 挨拶 greetings
aisatsu o suru 挨拶をする to greet
aisukurîmu アイスクリーム ice cream
aisuru 愛する to love
aji 味 taste
ajia アジア Asia
ajike no nai 味気のない dreary
ajimi o suru 味見をする to taste (salty, spicy)
akachan 赤ちゃん baby
akai 赤い red
akari 明かり light (noun)
akarui 明るい bright
akemashite omedetô 明けましておめでとう happy new year!
akeru 開ける to open
aki 秋 autumn, fall (season)
akichi 空き地 field, empty space
akiraka ni suru 明らかにする to reveal (make known)
akubisuru あくびする to yawn
akushû 悪臭 odor, bad smell
akushû o hanatsu 悪臭を放つ to stink
amai 甘い sweet
amakuchi shôyu 甘口しょう油 soy sauce (sweet)
amarini~sugiru あまりに～過ぎる too, excessively
amazuppai 甘酸っぱい sweet and sour
ame 飴 candy, sweets
ame 雨 rain
ame ga furu 雨が降る to rain
amerika アメリカ America
amerika gasshûkoku アメリカ合衆国 United States
amerika(jin) no アメリカ（人）の American
ami 網 net
ana 穴 hole
anata あなた you (familiar, female)
ani 兄 older brother
anka na 安価な inexpensive
annaijo 案内所 information booth
annainin 案内人 guide, lead
annaisuru 案内する to lead (to guide someone somewhere)
anzen na 安全な safe, secure
aoi 青い blue
aoyasai 青野菜 greens (vegetables)
apâto アパート flat, apartment
araarashii 荒々しい fierce

A

araiotosu 洗い落とす to scrub
arakajime あらかじめ beforehand, earlier
aramâ あらまあ goodness!
arappoi 荒っぽい rough
arashi 嵐 storm
arau 洗う to wash
arawareru 現れる to appear, to become visible
arawasu 現す to reveal (make visible)
are あれ that
arera あれら those
arigatô ありがとう thank you
arigatô to iu ありがとうと言う to say thank you
aruku 歩く to walk
asa 朝 morning
asai 浅い shallow
asatte 明後日 day after tomorrow
ase o kaku 汗をかく to sweat, to perspire
ashi 足 foot, 脚 leg
ashidori 足取り step
asobi mawaru 遊びまわる to play around
asu 明日 tomorrow
ataeru 与える to give
atama 頭 head
atarashii 新しい new
atatakai 暖かい warm
atatameru 温める to heat
atsui 厚い thick (of things)
atsui 熱い hot (temperature)
atsukau 扱う to treat
atsumeru 集める to assemble, to gather
atsuryoku 圧力 pressure
au 会う to meet
awaseru 合わせる to join, to go along
ayamaru 謝る to apologize, to say sorry
ayamatta 誤った wrong (false)
aza あざ bruise
azukeru 預ける to deposit (leave behind with someone)

B

bâ バー bar (serving drinks)
baffarô バッファロー buffalo (water buffalo)
bâgen バーゲン sale (reduced prices)
bai 倍 times (multiplying)
baiten 売店 stall (of vendor)
baketsu バケツ bucket
bakkin 罰金 fine (punishment)
banana バナナ banana
bangumi 番組 show (broadcast)
bankai 挽回 recovery
barabara ni suru ばらばらにする to break apart
basha 馬車 cart (horsecart)
basho 場所 place
basu バス bus
basukettobôru バスケットボール basketball
basurôbu バスローブ bathrobe
basutei バス停 bus station
batsu no warui ばつの悪い embarrassed, embarrassing
batâ バター butter
beddo ベッド bed
bengoshi 弁護士 lawyer
benkyôzukue 勉強机 desk
benri na 便利な convenient
beruto ベルト belt
besuto ベスト vest
besuto o tsukusu ベストを尽くす to do one's best
betonamu ベトナム Vietnam
betonamu(jin) no ベトナム（人）の Vietnamese

betsu no 別の another (different)
bîchi ビーチ beach
bideo dekki ビデオデッキ VCR
bideo kasetto ビデオカセット video cassette
bideo rekôdâ ビデオレコーダー video recorder
bikô 鼻腔 nostril
bin 瓶 bottle
binsoku ni 敏速に quickly
bîru ビール beer
biruma ビルマ（ミャンマーの旧称） Burma
biruma(jin) no ビルマ（人）の Burmese
bisuketto ビスケット biscuit
biza ビザ visa
bô 棒 stick, pole
bôeki 貿易 trade, exchange
bôgai 妨害 disturbance
bôgyosuru 防御する to defend
bon 盆 tray
bôru ボール ball
bôrugami ボール紙 cardboard
bôrupen ボールペン ballpoint pen
bôshi 帽子（つばの広い） hat
bôto ボート boat
bu 部 department
bubunteki ni 部分的に partly
budô 葡萄 grapes
buhin 部品 part (of machine)
bujoku 侮辱 insult
bujokusuru 侮辱する to insult
buki 武器 arm, weapon
bukkyô 仏教 Buddhism
bukkyôto 仏教徒 Buddhist
bun 文 sentence
bunbôgu 文房具 stationery
bungaku 文学 literature
bunka 文化 culture
bunkatsu 分割 division, split up
bunrui 分類 categorization
buntsûsuru 文通する to correspond (write letters)
burajâ ブラジャー bra
burashi ブラシ brush
burausu ブラウス blouse
burei 無礼 impolite
burokkorî ブロッコリー broccoli
burêki ブレーキ brake
burêki o kakeru ブレーキをかける to brake
burîfu ブリーフ（下着） briefs
burîfukêsu ブリーフケース briefcase
buta 豚 pig
butaniku 豚肉 pork
buttai 物体 object, thing
buzoku 部族 tribe
byô 秒 second
byôdô 平等 equality
byôin 病院 hospital
byôki 病気 disease, illness
byôki no 病気の ill, sick
byôshasuru 描写する to describe

C

cha 茶 tea
chairoi 茶色い brown (adjective)
chakurikusuru 着陸する（飛行機） to land (plane)
chawan 茶わん cup
chekku チェック checked pattern
chesu チェス chess
chi 血 blood
chichi 父 father
chiiki 地域 area, region
chijoku 恥辱 shame, disgrace
chikaku de 近くで around, nearby
chikara 力 force, power, strength
chikarazuyoi 力強い powerful
chikazuku 近づく（空間、時間） to approach (in space and time)

chikyû 地球 Earth
chîmu チーム team
chingashisuru 賃貸しする to rent out
chingin 賃金 wages
chippu チップ tip (gratuity)
chirakari 散かり in a mess
chiryô 治療（医療） cure (medical)
chiryôsuru 治療する to treat (medically)
chîsai 小さい little, small
chisei 知性 intelligence
chishiki 知識 knowledge
chishiki ga aru 知識がある to know, be acquainted with
chitsu 膣 vagina
chizu 地図 map
chîzu チーズ cheese
chokumensuru 直面する to face
chôbo 帳簿 account book
chôchô 蝶々 butterfly
chôhôkei 長方形 rectangle
chôji 丁子 cloves
chôjitabako 丁子タバコ clove cigarette
chôkakushôgai no 聴覚障害の deaf
chôkei 長兄 older brother
chokki チョッキ vest
chôkoku 彫刻 carving, sculpture
chôkokusuru 彫刻する to sculpt
chokorêto チョコレート chocolate
chôrisareta 調理された cooked
chôsasuru 調査する to examine
chôseisuru 調整する to organize, to arrange
chôsen 挑戦 challenge
chôshi 長姉 older sister
chôshoku 朝食 breakfast, morning meal
chôshoku o toru 朝食をとる to eat breakfast
chôwa no toreta 調和のとれた harmonious
chûgoku 中国 China
chûgoku(jin) no 中国（人）の Chinese
chûi 注意 notice
chûi o harau 注意を払う to pay attention
chûibukai 注意深い cautious
chûmoku 注目 notice
chûmon 注文 order (placed for food, goods)
chûmonsuru 注文する to order (something)
chûô 中央 middle, center
chûsha 注射 injection
chûshasuru 注射する to inject
chûshasuru 駐車する to park (car)
chûshin 中心 center, middle
chûshin no 中心の central
chûshoku 昼食 lunch, midday meal
chûshoku o toru 昼食をとる to eat lunch

D

daenkei no 楕円形の oval (shape)
dageki 打撃 hit, strike
daiben 大便 feces
daibubun wa 大部分は mostly
daidokoro 台所 kitchen
daigaku 大学 university
daimei 題名（本、映画） title (of book, film)
daisan no 第三の third
daitai だいたい more or less
daitôryô 大統領 president
daiyamondo ダイヤモンド diamond
dakara だから so, because of that
~dake de naku~mo mata 〜だけでなく〜もまた not only ... but also
damasu だます to cheat, to deceive

dame だめ don't!, no good
danbôru bako 段ボール箱 cardboard box
dango 団子 dumpling
danjikisuru 断食する to fast
dankotoshita 断固とした determined, stubborn, firm (definite)
dansei 男性 male
dare だれ who
dareka だれか anybody, anyone
dareka だれか somebody, someone
daremo~nai だれも～ない nobody
dâsu ダース dozen
datô na 妥当な adequate
~de ～で in, at
~de kenkasuru ～で喧嘩する to fight over
~de naikagiri ～でない限り unless
~de nakereba ～でなければ if not
~de warareta ～で割られた divided by
decchiageru でっち上げる to make up, invent
deguchi 出口 exit, way out
dekibae できばえ performance
dekigoto 出来事 event, happening, incident
~dekiru ～できる can, be able to
~demonai ～でもない nor, neither
dengon 伝言 message
denki 電気 electricity, light
denki kiki 電気機器 appliance, electrical
denki no 電気の electric
densetsu no 伝説の legend
densha 電車 train
denshi mêru 電子メール email (system, message)
denshi mêru adoresu 電子メールアドレス email address
denshi mêru o okuru 電子メールを送る to email
denshi no 電子の electronic
dentô 伝統 tradition
dentôteki na 伝統的な traditional
denwa 電話 telephone
denwa ni deru 電話にでる answer the phone
denwa o kakeru 電話をかける to dial (telephone)
denwa o suru 電話をする to call on the telephone
denwabangô 電話番号 telephone number
denwa no koki 子機（電話） extension (telephone)
denwasuru 電話する to ring (on the telephone)
depparu 出っ張る to stick out
depâtto デパート department store
deru 出る to go out, to exit
deshô ～でしょう probably
desuku デスク desk
dewa nai ～ではない no, not
dezâto デザート sweets, dessert
dîbuidî ディーブイディー DVD
dô 銅 bronze, copper
dôbutsu 動物 animal
dôbutsuen 動物園 zoo
dochiraka (ippô) no どちらか（一方）の either
dodai 土台 basis
dôgu 道具 tool, utensil, instrument
dôhansuru 同伴する to accompany
dôi 同意 agreement
dôisuru 同意する to agree
dôitashimashite どういたしまして don't mention it! you're welcome!
dôitsu no 同一の identical
dôji ni 同時に at the same time
dojô 土壌 earth, soil
doko どこ where

D

doko e どこへ where to
dokodemo どこでも everywhere, anywhere
dokoka どこか somewhere
dokonimo~nai どこにも〜ない nowhere
doku 毒 poison
dokuritsushita 独立した free, independent
dokusei no 毒性の poisonous
dokushin no 独身の single (not married)
dokutoku no 独特の characteristic
dôkyô 道教 Taoism
donburi どんぶり bowl
donna どんな what kind of
donokurai kakarimasu ka どのくらい掛かりますか（時間） how long does it take?
donokuraidesu ka どのくらいですか（数） how many?
donoyô ni どのように how
don'yorishita どんよりした（天気） dull (weather)
dore どれ which
doresu ドレス dress, frock
dorobô 泥棒 thief
doryoku 努力 effort
doryokusuru 努力する to make an effort, to try
dote 土手 bank (of river)
dôrinikanatteiru 道理にかなっている reasonable
dôryokusha 動力車 motor vehicle
dôryô 同僚 co-worker, colleague
dôyara~rashii どうやら〜らしい apparently
dôyô ni 同様に alike
dôzo どうぞ（勧めるとき） please (go ahead)
doyôbi 土曜日 Saturday

E

~e 〜へ（場所） to, toward
~e mukau 〜へ向かう to head for, toward
~e yôkoso 〜へようこそ welcome to
e 絵 picture
eakon エアコン air conditioning
ebi 海老 shrimp, prawn
eda 枝 branch
eien ni 永遠に for ever
eiga 映画 film, movie
eigakan 映画館 cinema, movie house
eikoku 英国 United Kingdom
eikoku(jin) no 英国（人）の British
eikyô 影響 effect, influence
eikyô o ataeru 影響を与える to affect, to influence
eikyû no 永久の permanent
eki 駅 train station
en 円 circle
endômame エンドウ豆 peas
enjin エンジン motor, engine
enjo 援助 assistance
enkai 宴会 banquet
enkatsu ni susumu 円滑にすすむ to go smoothly
enkishita 延期した postponed, delayed
enkisuru 延期する to postpone, to put off, to delay
enpitsu 鉛筆 pencil
erabu 選ぶ to pick, to choose, to select
erebêtâ エレベーター lift, elevator
eru 得る to earn
esukarêtâ エスカレーター escalator

F

fakkusu ファックス fax (machine)
fakkusu o okuru ファックスを送る to fax
fakkusubun ファックス文 fax (message)
fan ファン fan (admirer)
ferî フェリー ferry
firipin フィリピン Philippines
firumu フィルム film (camera)
fôku フォーク fork
fuhei 不平 complaint
fuhei o kobosu 不平をこぼす to complain
fuhitsuyô na 不必要な unnecessary
fuhô no 不法の illegal
fujin 婦人 lady
fukai 深い deep
fukanô na 不可能な impossible
fukô 不幸 misfortune
fukô na 不幸な unhappy
fuku 服 clothes, clothing
fuku o nugu 服を脱ぐ to get undressed
fukubu 腹部 abdomen
fukumu 含む to include
fukuzatsu na 複雑な complicated
fumô no 不毛の barren
fun 分 minute
funatabi o suru 船旅をする to sail
funbetsu no aru 分別のある reasonable (sensible)
fune 船 ship
funshitsubutsu 紛失物 lost property
fun'iki 雰囲気 atmosphere, ambience
furikaeru 振り返る to turn around
furo 風呂 bath
furoppîdisuku フロッピーディスク floppy disk
furu 振る to shake, to wave
furui 古い（物）old (of things)
furumau 振舞う to act, to behave
furûto, fue フルート、笛 flute
fusawashii ふさわしい suitable, fitting
fuseikaku na 不正確な inaccurate
fushô 負傷 injury
futa ふた lid
futatabi 再び again
futotta 太った fat, plump
fûtô 封筒 envelope
futsû 普通 normal
futsû wa 普通は normally, usually
futsûyûbin 普通郵便 surface mail
futtôsuru 沸騰する to boil
fuun 不運 bad luck
fuun na 不運な unlucky
fû o suru 封をする to steal
fuyasu 増やす to increase

G

ga 蛾 moth
~ga aru ～がある there is, there are
~ga hoshii ～が欲しい to want
~ga iru ～がいる there is, there are
gacchisuru 合致する to fit
gachô ガチョウ goose
gaido ガイド guide
gaikoku de 外国で abroad
gaikoku no 外国の foreign
gaikokujin 外国人 foreigner
gaitô 外套 coat, overcoat
gakkô 学校 school
gakudô 学童 schoolchild
gakusei 学生 student
gakushûsuru 学習する to study, to learn
gamen 画面 screen (of computer)
ganbô 願望 desire

G

ganko na 頑固な stubborn, determined
ganryô 顔料 paint
gara 柄 pattern, design
garasu ガラス glass (material)
gasorin ガソリン gasoline, petrol
gatsu 月 month
gaun ガウン dressing gown
geijutsu 芸術 art
geijutsuka 芸術家 artist
gekijo 劇場 theater (drama)
gekkei ga aru 月経がある to menstruate
gendai no 現代の modern
gengo 言語 language
genkan 玄関 entrance, way in, front door
genkei no 原型の original
genki 元気 how are you?
genki na 元気な fine, energetic
genki ni naru 元気になる to get better
genkin 現金 cash, money
genshô 減少 reduction
genzai 現在 presently, nowadays
genzai no 現在の current
genzôsuru 現像する to develop (film)
gen'in 原因 cause
getsuyôbi 月曜日 Monday
gikei 義兄 brother-in-law (older sister's husband or wife's older brother)
gimai 義妹 sister-in-law (younger brother's wife or husband's younger sister)
gimu 義務 duty (responsibility)
gimuteki na 義務的な compulsory
gin 銀 silver
ginkô 銀行 bank (finance)
giri no chichi 義理の父 father-in-law
giri no haha 義理の母 mother-in-law
giri no musuko 義理の息子 son-in-law
giri no musume 義理の娘 daughter-in-law
giron 議論 argument, discussion
gironsuru 議論する to argue, to discuss
gisei 犠牲 sacrifice
gisei ni suru 犠牲にする to sacrifice
gishi 義姉 sister-in-law (older brother's wife or husband's older sister)
gishiki 儀式 ceremony
gitei 義弟 brother-in-law (younger sister's husband or wife's younger brother)
go 五 five
go 語 word
gochisô ご馳走 treat (something special), delicious meal
gofujin ご婦人（女性への敬称） madam (term of address)
gogatsu 五月 May
gogo 午後 p.m.
gohan ご飯（炊いた） rice (cooked)
gôhô no 合法の legal
gojû 五十 fifty
gokai 誤解 misunderstanding
gôkakusuru 合格する（試験） to pass (exam)
gôka na 豪華な luxurious
gôkei no 合計の total
goma ゴマ sesame seeds
goma abura ゴマ油 sesame oil
gomennasai ごめんなさい sorry! excuse me!
gomi ごみ garbage
gomu ゴム rubber
goraku 娯楽 pastime
gôru ゴール goal
gorufu ゴルフ golf

gôsei no 合成の synthetic
gotakô o inorimasu ご多幸を祈ります best wishes
~gotoni 〜毎に each, every
guntai 軍隊 army, troops
gurasu グラス glass (for drinking)
guratsuita ぐらついた loose (wobbly)
gurûpu グループ group
gûzen ni 偶然に accidentally, by chance
gûzô 偶像 idol
gyakkôsuru 逆行する to go backwards
gyanburu ギャンブル gamble
gyoshô 魚醤 fish sauce
gyôgi no ii 行儀のいい well-behaved, well-mannered
gyôretsu 行列 line (queue)
gyûniku 牛肉 beef
gyûnyû 牛乳 milk

H

ha 歯 teeth, tooth
ha 葉 leaf
haba 幅 width
habahiroi 幅広い wide
haburashi 歯ブラシ toothbrush
hachi 八 eight
hachi 鉢 pot
hachigatsu 八月 August
hachijû 八十 eighty
hachimitsu 蜂蜜 honey
hada 肌 skin
hadagi 肌着 underwear
hadaka no 裸の naked, nude
hâdodisuku ハードディスク hard disk
hae 蝿 fly (insect)
haeru 生える to grow, to come out
hagaki 葉書 postcard
hagane はがね steel
hageshiku utsu 激しく打つ to beat (to strike)
hageta はげた bald
haha 母 mother
hai はい yes
hai 肺 lungs
haibensuru 排便する to defecate
haigûsha 配偶者 spouse
haiiro no 灰色の grey
hairu 入る to enter
haitatsusuru 配達する to deliver
haji 端 tip (end)
hajimari 始まり start, beginning
hajime ni 初めに at first
hajimeru 始める to begin, to start
hajite 恥じて ashamed, embarrassed
haka 墓 grave
hakaisareta 破壊された destroyed, ruined
hakaisuru 破壊する to destroy
hakari はかり scales
hakariwakeru 計り分ける to measure out
hakariwakeru 量り分ける to weigh out
hakaru 計る to measure
hakaru 量る to weigh
hakarukoto 計ること measurement
hakidasu 吐き出す to vomit, spit out
hakike ga suru 吐き気がする to feel sick
hakkan 発汗 sweat
hakkensuru 発見する to discover
hako 箱 box
hakobu 運ぶ to carry
haku 掃く to sweep
hakusai 白菜 Chinese cabbage
hamabe 浜辺 beach
hamaki 葉巻 cigar
hamigakiko 歯磨き粉 toothpaste

hana 花 flower
hana 鼻 nose
hanabi 花火 fireworks
hanamuko 花婿 bridegroom
hanashi 話 story (tale)
hanashichû 話し中（電話）busy, engaged (telephone)
hanasu 話す to speak, to talk, to tell
hanayome 花嫁 bride
hanbun 半分 half
hankagai 繁華街 downtown, center (of city)
hankyôsuru 反響する to reflect
hannô 反応 reaction, response
hannôsuru 反応する to react
hansamu ハンサム handsome
hantai no 反対の opposed, opposite
hantaisuru 反対する to object, to protest, to oppose
hanzaisha 犯罪者 criminal
hara 腹 stomach, belly
harau 払う to pay
hareta 晴れた（天気）clear (of weather)
hari 針 needle
haru 春 spring (season)
hasami はさみ scissors
hashi 橋 bridge
hashi 端 edge, end (tip)
hashi 箸 chopsticks
hashigo 梯子 ladder
hashira 柱 post, column, pillar
hashiru 走る to run
hata 旗 flag
hatasu 果たす fulfill
hatsugen 発言 utterance
hatsumei 発明 invitation
hatsumeisuru 発明する to invent
hatsunetsu 発熱 fever
hatsuonsuru 発音する to pronounce
hatten 発展 development
hattensuru 発展する to develop
hayai 速い fast, rapid
hayakunaotte 早く治って get well soon!
hazukashii 恥ずかしい embarrassing
hebi 蛇 snake
heibon na 平凡な plain (not fancy)
heikin 平均 average (numbers)
heisa 閉鎖（道）closed (road)
heitai 兵隊 soldier
heitan na 平坦な flat, smooth
heiten 閉店（店）closed (shop)
heiwa 平和 peace
heiwa na 平和な peaceful
hen na 変な strange
henji 返事 answer, response (spoken), reply
henji o suru 返事をする to answer, to reply
henshin 返信 answer, response (written)
henshinsuru 返信する to answer, to respond (written)
hentô 返答 response
hentôsuru 返答する to reply (in speech), to respond
herasu 減らす to reduce
heru 減る to decrease
heya 部屋 room
hi ga tsuku 火がつく to be caught on fire
hiatari ga ii 日当たりがいい sunny
hidarigawa 左側 left-hand side
hidoi ひどい terrible
higashi 東 east
hiji ひじ elbow
hijikakeisu ひじ掛け椅子 armchair
hijô ni 非常に very, extremely
hikaeme na 控えめな modest
hikakusuru 比較する to compare
hikaru 光る to shine
hikidashi 引き出し drawer

hikô 飛行 flight
hikôki 飛行機 aeroplane, airplane
hiku 引く to pull, to draw
hikui 低い low, short (not tall)
himitsu 秘密 secret
himitsu o mamoru 秘密を守る to keep a secret
himo 紐 string
hinan 非難（言葉で）attack (with words), blame
hinmoku 品目 item, individual thing
hinode 日の出 sunrise
hinoiri 日の入 sunset
hinpan ni 頻繁に frequently
hiraiteiru 開いている open
hiroba 広場 square, town square
hirobiroshita 広々した spacious
hiroi 広い broad, spacious, large
hiroma 広間 hall
hishaku ひしゃく dipper, ladle
hisho 秘書 secretary
hissu no 必須の compulsory
hitaru 浸る to soak
hîta 引いた less, minus
hito 人 person
hitobito 人々 people
hitokire 一切れ piece, portion
hitonami 人並み average (so-so, just okay)
hitori ひとりで alone, on one's own
hitsuji 羊 sheep
hitsujiniku 羊肉 lamb, mutton
hitsuyô na 必要な necessary
hitsuyô de aru 必要である to need
hitsuyôsei 必要性 necessity
hiyasareta 冷やされた chilled
hiyoku na 肥沃な fertile
hiyô 費用 cost (expense)
hiza 膝 knee
hizashi 日差し sunlight
hizuke 日付 date (of the month)
hô 頬 cheek
hôgen 方言 dialect
hogoku 保護区（動物）reserve (for animals)
hoka no ほかの different, other
hokansuru 保管する to leave behind for safekeeping
hoken 保険 insurance
hokori 誇り pride
hokori 埃 dust
hokori ni omou 誇りに思う to be proud
hokôkyori 歩行距離 distance that one walks
hokusei 北西 north-west
hokutô 北東 north-east
hon 本 book
hone 骨 bone
honkon 香港 Hong Kong
honô 炎 fire
hontô 本当 really, truth
hontô ni 本当に really, truly
hontô no 本当の true
honyaku 翻訳 translation
horaana 洞穴 cave
horu 彫る to carve
hoshi 星 star
hoshôsho 保証書 guarantee
hoshôsuru 保証する to guarantee
hosoi 細い slender, slim
hoteru ホテル hotel
hotondo ほとんど almost, most (the most of), nearly
hotondo~nai ほとんど〜ない hardly, seldom
hôhô 方法 method, way
hôki ほうき broom
hôkisuru 放棄する to desert, to abandon
hôkoku 報告 report
hôkokusuru 報告する to report
hôkô 方向 direction

hôrensô ほうれん草 spinach
hôritsu 法律 laws, legislation
hôsekirui 宝石類 jewellery
hôshi 奉仕 service
hôsô 放送 broadcast, program
hôsômô 放送網 network
hôsôsuru 放送する to broadcast
hôtai 包帯 bandage
hozonsareta 保存された cured, preserved
hyakkaten 百貨店 department store
hyaku 百 hundred
hyakubunritsu 百分率 percent, percentage
hyakuman 百万 million
hyô 表 list
hyômen 表面 surface
hyôshiki 標識 sign, signpost
hyottoshitara~kamoshirenai ひょっとしたら〜かもしれない could, might

I

ichi 一 one
ichiba 市場 market
ichiban no 一番の first
ichibu 一部 part (not whole)
ichido 一度 once
ichigatsu 一月 January
ichihôkô o shimesu 位置方角を示す point out the position/direction
ichijiteki na 一時的な temporary
ichimai no kami 一枚の紙 a sheet of paper
ichiman 一万 ten thousand
idaku 抱く to embrace
ido 井戸 well (for water)
idôsuru 移動する to move
ie 家 home, house
ie de 家で at home
igaku no 医学の medical
igirisu イギリス England, UK
igirisu(jin) no イギリス（人）の English, British
ijiwarui 意地悪い mean (cruel)
ika イカ squid
ikari 怒り anger
iken 意見 opinion
ikinobiru 生延びる to survive
ikite 生きて alive
ikiteiru 生きている living
ikko no 一個の a piece of
iku 行く to go
ikuradesuka いくらですか（価格） how much?
ikutsudesuka いくつですか（年齢） how old?
ikutsuka no いくつかの several, some
ima 今 now
imi 意味 meaning
imisuru 意味する to mean (word)
imôto 妹 younger sister
inaka 田舎 country (rural area)
inazuma 稲妻 lightning
indoneshia インドネシア Indonesia
indoneshia(jin) no インドネシア（人）の Indonesian
ine 稲 rice (plant)
ingenmame インゲン豆 kidney beans
inoru 祈る to pray
insatsusuru 印刷する to print
inshôzukeru 印象付ける to make an impression
intaishita 引退した retired
intânetto インターネット Internet
inu 犬 dog
ippai no いっぱいの full of
ippakusuru 一泊する to stay overnight
ippan ni 一般に generally

ippanteki na 一般的な general, all-purpose
irai 以来 since
iraisuru 依頼する to ask for, to request
irekawaru 入れ替わる to replace
iriguchi 入り口 entrance, way in
iro 色 color
irui 衣類 garment
isamashii 勇ましい brave, daring
iseki 遺跡 remains (historical)
isha 医者 doctor
ishi 石 rock, stone
isogashii 忙しい busy (doing something)
isoide 急いで in a hurry
isshô 一生 lifetime
issô いっそう even (also)
isu 椅子 chair, seat
isuramu no イスラムの Islamic
isuramukyô no イスラム教（徒）の Muslim
itai 痛い sore, painful
itami 痛み ache, pain
itamu 痛む to ache
itazurana いたずらな naughty
ito 意図 intention
ito 糸 thread
itosareta 意図された intended for
itsu いつ when
itsudemo いつでも whenever
itsumo いつも always, every-time
itsumo no いつもの usual
ittsui no 一対の a pair of
iu 言う to say
iwau 祝う to celebrate
iyakuhin 医薬品 medicine
iyaringu イヤリング earrings
izen ni 以前に before (in time)
izonsuru 依存する to depend on

J

jagaimo ジャガイモ potato
jaketto ジャケット coat, jacket
jama 邪魔 hindrance
jamu ジャム jam
janguru ジャングル jungle
jibun no 自分の own, personal
jidôsha 自動車 automobile, car
jidôshashûrikôjô 自動車修理工場 garage (for repairs)
jijitsu 事実 fact
jiin 寺院 temple
jikaku 自覚 awareness
jikakusuru 自覚する to be conscious of
jikan 時間 hour, time
jikandôri ni 時間どおりに punctual, on time
jiken 事件 incident
jiko 事故 accident
jikokuhyô 時刻表 timetable
jikoshôkaisuru 自己紹介する to introduce oneself
jimen 地面 ground, earth
jimi na 地味な simple, plain (modest)
jimusho 事務所 office
jinkô 人口 population
jinkô no 人工の artificial
jinrui 人類 human
jinzô 腎臓 kidney
jishin 自信 confidence
jishin 自身 self
jishin 地震 earthquake
jishin o motsu 自信を持つ to have confidence
jisho 辞書 dictionary
jisonshin 自尊心 pride
jissai ni 実際に actually, really (in fact)
jiten 時点（時間）point (in time)
jitensha 自転車 bicycle

J

jitsugyôka 実業家 businessperson
jiyû 自由 freedom
jô 錠 lock
jô no kakatta 錠の掛かった locked
jô o kakeru 錠を掛ける to lock
jôdan 冗談 joke
jogen 助言 advice
jogensuru 助言する to advise
jôhô 情報 information
jôi no 上位の ranked higher
jojo ni 徐々に gradually
jôkai e 上階へ upstairs
jôken 条件 condition (pre-condition)
jôki 蒸気 steam
jôku ジョーク joke
jôkyaku 乗客 passenger
jôkyô 状況 condition (status), situation, how things are
joô 女王 queen
jôryûshu 蒸留酒 spirits, hard liquor
josei 女性 female, woman
jôsharyôkin 乗車料金 fare
jôshasuru 乗車する to get on, to ride, to board
jôshi 上司 boss
jôshô 上昇 rise, ascendance
jôzai 錠剤 pills, tablets
jû 十 ten
jûbun na 十分な enough
jûgatsu 十月 October
jûgo 十五 fifteen
jugyô 授業 lesson, class
jûhachi 十八 eighteen
jûichi 十一 eleven
jûichigatsu 十一月 November
jûjun na 従順な obedient, tame
jukurenshita 熟練した skillful
jukushita 熟した ripe
jukyô 儒教 Confucianism
jûkyû 十九 nineteen
jûman 十万 hundred thousand
jûnana 十七 seventeen
junban 順番 order, sequence
junbisuru 準備する to prepare, to make ready
junchô na 順調な smooth, normal
jûni 十二 twelve
jûnigatsu 十二月 December
jûnin 住人 resident, inhabitant
junjo 順序 sequence, order
junsui na 純粋な pure
jûoku 十億 billion
juritsusuru 樹立する to establish, to set up
jûroku 十六 sixteen
jûsan 十三 thirteen
jûshichi 十七 seventeen
jûsho 住所 address
jûsu ジュース juice
jûtan 絨毯 carpet
jûyaku 重役（会社の）director (of company)
jûyon 十四 fourteen
jûyô na 重要な major (important)
jûyô sa 重要さ importance

K

ka 蚊 mosquito
kaban 鞄 bag
kabe 壁 wall
kabi カビ mold, mildew
kabin 花瓶 vase
kachi 価値 value (cost)
kado 角 corner
kaeru 変える to change
kaesu 返す to return, to give back
kagaku 科学 science
kagami 鏡 mirror
kage 陰 shade
kage 影 shadow
kagee 影絵 shadow play
kagi 鍵（部屋）key (to room)
kago かご basket

kagu 家具 furniture
kai 階（建物）storey (of a building)
kaichô 会長 president
kaichûdentô 懐中電灯 flashlight, torch
kaidan 階段 steps, stairs
kaifukushita 回復した recovered, cured
kaiga 絵画 painting
kaigai no 海外の overseas
kaigô 会合 meeting
kaihatsu 開発 development
kaiin 会員 member
kaika ni 階下に downstairs
kaiketsusuru 解決する（問題） to resolve, to solve (a problem)
kaikosuru 解雇する to fire someone
kaikyô 海峡 strait
kaikyû 階級 rank, station in life
kaimono o suru 買い物をする to go shopping, to shop
kairomô 回路網 network
kaisanbutsu 海産物 seafood
kaisha 会社 company
kaiwa 会話 conversation
kaji o toru かじをとる to steer
kajû 果汁 juice
kakaku 価格 price
kakegoto 賭け事 gamble
kaketeiru 欠けている lacking
kaki 牡蠣 oyster
kakikomu 書き込む to fill out (form)
kakitome 書留 registered post
kakitomeru 書き留める to note down
kakôsuru 下降する to descend, to go/come down
kaku 書く（手紙、本、音楽） to write (letters, books, music)
kaku 描く（絵）to paint, (a painting)
kakuchôsuru 拡張する to enlarge
kakudaisuru 拡大する to expand, to grow larger
kakureta 隠れた hidden
kakushin 確信 conviction
kakusu 隠す to hide
kakuteishita 確定した definite
kamaboko かまぼこ fish paste
kamado かまど cooker
kamera カメラ camera
kami 紙 paper
kami 神 God
kami 髪 hair
kamikazari 髪飾り headdress
kaminari 雷 thunder
~kamoshirenai 〜かもしれない maybe
kamu 噛む to bite, to chew
kan 缶 can, tin
kanari かなり quite (fairly)
kanari no かなりの fair
kanashii 悲しい sad, unhappy
kanashimi 悲しみ sorrow
kanban 看板 signboard
kanbatsu 干ばつ drought
kanbojia カンボジア Cambodia
kanbojia(jin) no カンボジア（人）の Cambodian
kanchisuru 完治する to fully recover
kandai na 寛大な generous
kandai sa 寛大さ generosity
kane 金 money
kane o nakusu 金をなくす to lose money
kanemochi 金持ち rich person
kangae 考え idea
kangaeru 考える to ponder, to think
kani 蟹 crab
kanja 患者 patient (doctor's)
kanji 感じ feeling

K

JAPANESE—ENGLISH

K

kanjiru 感じる to feel
kanjô 感情 emotion
kanjô o gaisuru 感情を害する to hurt one's feeling
kanjôdai 勘定台 counter (for paying, buying tickets)
kankinsuru 換金する to exchange (money)
kankitsurui かんきつ類 citrus
kankoku 韓国 South Korea
kankoku(jin) no 韓国（人）の South Korean
kankô 観光 sightseeing
kankôkyaku 観光客 tourist
kankyô 環境 environment, surroundings
kanningu カンニング cheating
kanô na 可能な possible
kanô ni suru 可能にする to make possible
kanojo 彼女 girlfriend
kanojo ha 彼女は she
kanojo no 彼女の hers
kanojo o 彼女を her
kanpai 乾杯 cheers!
kanpeki na 完璧な complete (thorough)
kanrinin 管理人 custodian
kanseishita 完成した complete (finished)
kanshasuru 感謝する to be grateful, to thank
kansôshita 乾燥した（天気） dry (weather)
kantan na 簡単な simple (easy)
kanyoshita 関与した involved
kanzei 関税 duty (import tax)
kanzen na 完全な whole, complete
kanzen ni 完全に completely, entirely
kanzen ni suru 完全にする to make whole
kanzô 肝臓 liver
kao 顔 face
kao o shikameru 顔をしかめる to frown
kao o shikameta 顔をしかめた with a frown
~kara 〜から from
~kara hazureru 〜からはずれる to come off
~kara okoru 〜から起こる originate, come from
~kara~ni idôsuru 〜から〜に移動する move from one place to
kara no 空の empty
karada 体 body
karai 辛い hot (spicy)
kare no 彼の his
kare o 彼を him
kare wa 彼は he
karera no 彼らの their, theirs
karera o 彼らを them
karera wa 彼らは they
kareshi 彼氏 boyfriend
kari ga aru 借りがある to owe
karifurawâ カリフラワー cauliflower
kariru 借りる to borrow
karôjite かろうじて barely
karui 軽い light (not heavy)
kasa 傘 umbrella
kasetto カセット cassette
kashi 菓子 confectionery
kashikoi 賢い clever, smart
kashitsu 過失 fault
kasu 貸す to lend, to rent
kata 肩 shoulder
katachi 形 form, shape, style
katachizukuru 形作る to form, to shape
katagaki 肩書き（人） title (of person)
katai 堅い stiff
katai 固い hard (solid)

katai 硬い（マットレス）firm (mattress)
katamichikippu 片道切符 one-way ticket
katazukeru 片付ける to tidy up
katei shitemiru 仮定してみる to hypothesize
kâten カーテン curtain
kâto カート（手押し）cart (pushcart)
katsudô 活動 activity
katsuryoku 活力 energy
katsute かつて in the past
kau 買う to buy
kauntâ カウンター counter (for paying, buying tickets)
kawa 川 river
kawa 革 leather
kawaii かわいい cute, appealing
kawairashii かわいらしい（女性）pretty (of women)
kawaita 乾いた dry
kawakasu 乾かす to dry
kawaru 変わる（状況が）to change (conditions, situations)
kawase sôba 為替相場 exchange rate
kawaserêto 為替レート rate of exchange (for foreign currency)
kayôbi 火曜日 Tuesday
kazan 火山 volcano
kazaru 飾る to decorate
kaze 風邪 cold, flu
kazoeru 数える to count, to reckon
kazoku 家族 family
kazu 数 number
ka~ ～か～ or
kega 怪我 wound
keihi 経費 expenses
keikaku 計画 plan, schedule
keikakusuru 計画する to plan
keiken 経験 experience
keikensuru 経験する to experience, to undergo
keikoku 警告 warning
keikokusuru 警告する to warn
keimusho 刑務所 jail, prison
keisanki 計算機 calculator
keisansuru 計算する to calculate
keisatsukan 警察官 police officer
keisatsu 警察 police
keitaidenwa 携帯電話 cell phone
keizai 経済 economy
keizaiteki na 経済的な economical
keizokusuru 継続する to continue
kekka 結果 result
kekkonshiki 結婚式 wedding
kekkonshita 結婚した married
kekkonsuru 結婚する to marry, to get married
kemuri 煙 smoke
ken 券（娯楽）ticket (for entertainment)
ken 腱 tendon
kenchiku 建築 architecture
kengi 嫌疑 suspicion
ken'i 権威 authority (person in charge)
kenka けんか fight, quarrel
kenkôteki na 健康的な healthy
kenkyû 研究 research
kenkyûsuru 研究する to research
kenri 権利 rights
kenryoku(sha) 権力（者）authority (power)
kensakusuru 検索する（本を）to look up (find in book)
ken'okan 嫌悪感 hatred
ken'osuru 嫌悪する to hate
keshiki 景色 scenery, view, panorama
keshita 消した off (turned off)
kesseki no 欠席の missing, absent
kesshin 決心 decision

kesshite~nai 決して〜ない never
kesu 消す to turn off
kesu 消す（火、ろうそく）to put out (fire, candle)
ketten 欠点 defect
ki 木 tree, wood
kî キー（コンピューター）key (computer)
ki o tsukete 気をつけて take care
kibin na 機敏な quick
kibishii きびしい severe, strict
kibô 希望 desire
kîbôdo キーボード（コンピューター）keyboard (of computer)
kichintoshita きちんとした neat, orderly
kiga 飢餓 famine
kigaeru 着替える to change clothes
kigan(suruhito) 祈願（する人）prayer
kigen 起源 origin
kigyô 企業 firm, company
kihon 基本 basic
kiji 記事 article (in newspaper)
kika 貴下（男性への敬称） sir (term of address)
kikai 機会 chance, opportunity
kikai 機械 machine
kikairui 機械類 machinery
kikan 期間 period (of time)
kiken 危険 danger
kiken na 危険な dangerous
kikô 気候 climate
kiku 聴く to listen
kiku 聞く to hear
kikyôsuru 帰郷する to return to one's town
kimeru 決める to decide, to fix
kimi 君 you (male)
kinben na 勤勉な hardworking, industrious
kinchôshita 緊張した tense
kinenhi 記念碑 monument
kiniiru 気に入る to suit one's taste
kininaru 気になる to be anxious
kinishinaide 気にしないで never mind!
kinjirareta 禁じられた forbidden
kinkyûjitai 緊急事態 emergency
kinkyû no 緊急の urgent
kinniku 筋肉 muscle
kinô 昨日 yesterday
kinoko きのこ mushroom
kinôsuru 機能する to function, to work
kinshisuru 禁止する to forbid
kinu 絹 silk
kinyôbi 金曜日 Friday
kioku 記憶 memories
kippu 切符（乗り物）ticket (for transport)
kirei na きれいな clean, beautiful
kireinisuru きれいにする to clean
kireme 切れめ cut, slice
kiri 霧 fog, mist
kirisutokyô キリスト教 Christianity
kirisutokyô(to) no キリスト教（徒）の Christian
kiroguramu キログラム kilogram
kîroi 黄色い yellow (adjective)
kiromêtâ キロメーター kilometer
kiru 切る to cut
kiru 着る to get dressed, to wear, to put on
kisetsu 季節 season
kisha 記者 journalist
kiso 基礎 base, foundation
kisoku 規則 rules
kisu キス kiss
kisu o suru キスをする to kiss
kita 北 north
kitachôsen 北朝鮮 North Korea
kitachôsen(jin) no 北朝鮮（人）の North Korean
kitai o motte 期待をもって hopefully

kitakusuru 帰宅する to go home
kitanai 汚い dirty
kitsui きつい close together, tight
kitte 切手（郵便） stamp (postage)
kîwifurûtsu キーウィフルーツ kiwi fruit
kiyomeru 清める to purify
kizamu 刻む to engrave
kizuiteiru 気づいている aware
kizuku 気づく to notice
kizutsuita 傷ついた hurt, injured
kizutsuku 傷つく to get hurt/injured
kodai no 古代の ancient
kôdô 行動 action
kodomo 子供（子孫/若い人一般） child (offspring/young person)
koe 声 voice
kôen 公園 garden, park
kôen 公演 performance
kôfunshita 興奮した on (turned on), excited
kôgaku no 高額の expensive
kôgan 睾丸 testicles
kogatabasu 小型バス minibus
kogatana 小刀 knife
kôgei 工芸 crafts
kôgeika 工芸家 craftsperson
kôgeki 攻撃（戦争） attack (in war)
kôgi 講義 lecture
kogirei na こぎれいな（場所、物） neat (of places, things)
kogitte o kankinsuru 小切手を換金する to cash a check
kôhei na 公平な just, fair
kôhî コーヒー coffee
koi 濃い thick (of liquids)
koishikuomou 恋しく思う to miss (loved one)
koji 古寺 ancient temple
kojinteki na 個人的な private
kôjô 工場 factory
kôka 硬貨 coin
kôkai 後悔 regret
kôkaisuru 後悔する to regret
kôkan 交換 exchange
kôkansuru 交換する to switch, to change
kokka 国家 country (nation)
kokku コック cook (person)
kokkyô 国境 border (between countries)
koko ここ here
koko ni iru ここにいる to be present (here)
kokochiyoi 心地良い comfortable
kokonattsu ココナッツ coconut
kokoromi 試み attempt
kokoromiru 試みる to attempt
kokorozuke 心付け tip (gratuity)
kôkûbin 航空便 airmail
kokuin 刻印 stamp (ink)
kokusaiteki na 国際的な international
kokuseki 国籍 nationality
kôkyô no 公共の public
kome 米（穀物） rice (uncooked grains)
komichi 小道 alley, lane
kômon 肛門 anus
komugiko 小麦粉 flour
konagona ni kowareta 粉々に壊れた broken, shattered
konagona ni suru 粉々にする to shatter
konban 今晩 tonight
konchû 昆虫 insect
kone コネ contact, connection
kongansuru 懇願する to plead
kongôshita 混合した mixed
kon'nan na 困難な hard (difficult)
kon'nan 困難 trouble, difficulty
kon'nichi de wa 今日では nowadays
kon'nichiwa こんにちは hello, hi

K

kon'nichiwa to iu こんにちはと言う to say hello
kono この this (adjective)
konomanai 好まない to dislike
konomi ni urusai 好みにうるさい fussy
konomu 好む to prefer
kononde 好んで fond of
konpyûtâ コンピューター computer
konpôbako 梱包箱 crate
konranshita 混乱した confused
konro コンロ stove
kontei 根底 bottom (base)
konwakusaseru 困惑させる to confuse
konwakushita 困惑した confused, puzzled
kon'yakuchû no 婚約中の engaged (to be married)
kon'yakusha 婚約者 fiancé, fiancée
konzatsushita 混雑した crowded
koppu コップ cup
kopî コピー photocopy
kopîsuru コピーする to photocopy
korera no これらの these (adjective)
koriandâ コリアンダー（香草） cilantro, coriander
kôri 氷 ice
kôritsuku 凍りつく to freeze
korobu 転ぶ to fall over
korosu 殺す to kill, to murder
kôryosuru 考慮する to consider (to think over)
kôsaisuru 交際する to associate
kosame 小雨 shower (of rain)
kôsaten 交差点 intersection
kosei 個性 personality
kôshasuru 降車する to get off (transport)
kôshi 格子 bar (blocking way)
kôshi 講師（大学の） lecturer (at university)
koshikake 腰掛 stool
kôshiki no 公式の official, formal
kôshinryô 香辛料 spices
koshôsuru 故障する to break down (car, machine)
kôsui 香水 perfume
kotai no 固体の solid
kôtta 凍った frozen
koteisareta 固定された fixed, won't move
koto こと (intangible) thing, matter
kôto コート coat, overcoat
kotowaru 断る to decline (refuse)
kottôhin 骨董品 antiques
kôtsû 交通 traffic
kôun 幸運 lucky
kôun o inoru 幸運を祈る good luck!
kôunnimo 幸運にも fortunately
kowagatte 恐がって afraid
kowareta 壊れた broken, does not work, spoiled
koya 小屋 hut, shack
koyû no 固有の indigenous, peculiar
kozeni 小銭 small change
kôzui 洪水 flood
kozutsumi 小包 package, parcel
kubi 首 neck
kubikazari 首飾り necklace
kuchi 口 mouth
kuchibiru 唇 lips
kuchihige 口ひげ moustache
kudaketa 砕けた cracked
kudamono 果物 fruit
kûfuku no 空腹の hungry
kugatsu 九月 September
kugi 釘 nail (spike)
kujô 苦情 complaint
kûkan 空間 room, space
kûki 空気 air

kukkî クッキー biscuit (cookie)
kûkô 空港 airport
kumiawaseru 組み合わせる to assemble, to put together
kumotta 曇った overcast, cloudy
kuni 国 nation, country
kuni no 国の national
kunren 訓練 training
kurai 暗い dark
kurakkâ クラッカー cracker
kurasu クラス class
kurikaesu 繰り返す to repeat
kuroi 黒い black
kurokoshô 黒胡椒 pepper, black
kuromame 黒豆 black beans
kuru 来る to come
kurubushi くるぶし ankle
kuruma ni noseru 車に乗せる（人を）to pick up (someone)
kurushimi 苦しみ suffering
kurushimu 苦しむ to suffer
kurutta 狂った crazy
kusa 草 grass
kusai 臭い smelly
kusatta 腐った rotten, spoiled
kushami くしゃみ sneeze
kushami o suru くしゃみをする to sneeze
kushi 櫛 comb
kuso くそ shit
kûsô 空想 fancy, fantasy
kûsôsuru 空想する to daydream
kusuri 薬 drug (medicine)
kutôten 句読点 period (end of a sentence)
kutsu 靴 shoes
kutsurogu くつろぐ to relax
kutsushita 靴下 socks
kuwaete 加えて in addition
kyabetsu キャベツ cabbage
kyaku 客 guest, customer
kyodai na 巨大な huge
kyoka 許可 permit, license
kyokasuru 許可する to let, to allow, to permit
kyokutan ni 極端に extremely
kyori 距離 distance
kyô 今日 today
kyôbai ni kakerareta 競売にかけられた auctioned off
kyôbai ni kakeru 競売にかける to auction
kyôdai きょうだい sibling, brothers
kyôdôkeieisha 共同経営者 partner (in business)
kyôhakusuru 脅迫する to threaten
kyôiku 教育 education
kyôikusuru 教育する to educate
kyôkai 教会 church
kyôkaisen 境界線 boundary, border
kyôki no 狂気の insane
kyômi bukai 興味深い interesting
kyôsô 競争 competition
kyôsôaite 競争相手 rival
kyôsôsuru 競争する to compete
kyozetsu 拒絶 refusal
kyû 九 nine
kyû ni 急に suddenly
kyûji 給仕 waiter, waitress
kyûjitu 休日 day off
kyûjosuru 救助する to rescue
kyûjû 九十 ninety
kyûka 休暇 holiday (vacation)
kyûri キュウリ cucumber
kyûryô 給料 salary
kyûyujo 給油所 gasoline station, petrol station

M

ma ni awase no 間に合わせの makeshift
macchi マッチ matches
machi 町 town

M

machigaerareta 間違えられた mistaken
machigai 間違い error
machigatta 間違った wrong (mistaken)
mada まだ still, even now
madadesu まだです not yet
mada~nai まだ〜ない not yet
~made 〜まで until
mae ni 前に before, in the past
maebaraisuru 前払いする to pay in advance
maemotte 前もって earlier, beforehand
magaru 曲がる to turn, to make a turn
magirawashii 紛らわしい confusing
mago 孫 grandchild
magomusuko 孫息子 grandson
magomusume 孫娘 granddaughter
mahishita 麻痺した numb
maikurobasu マイクロバス minibus
mainichi no 毎日の daily
maishû no 毎週の weekly
mâjan 麻雀 mahjong
majime na まじめな serious (not funny)
makeru 負ける to lose, to be defeated
makura 枕 pillow
mame 豆 bean
mamoru 守る to guard, to protect
mango マンゴ mango
manzokusaseru 満足させる to satisfy
manzokushita 満足した pleased, satisfied
mare ni まれに occasionally
marêshia マレーシア Malaysia
marêshia(jin) no マレーシア（人）の Malaysian
marui 丸い round (shape)
massâji マッサージ massage
massugu mae ni 真っ直ぐ前に straight ahead
massugu na 真っ直ぐな straight (not crooked)
masuku マスク mask
maton マトン mutton
matsu 待つ to wait for
matsuri 祭り festival
matto マット mat
mattoresu マットレス mattress
mausu マウス（コンピューター） mouse (computer)
mayaku 麻薬 drug, narcotic
mayonaka 真夜中 midnight
mayotta 迷った（道に） lost (can't find way)
mayuge 眉毛 eyebrow
mazaru 混ざる to mix
mazushii 貧しい poor
me 目 eye
megami 女神 goddess
megane めがね eyeglasses, spectacles
me ga samete 目が覚めて awake
mei 姪 niece
meirei 命令 command, order
meireisuru 命令する to order, to command
meiwaku 迷惑 bother, nuisance
meiwakusuru 迷惑する to be annoyed
meiwaku o kakeru 迷惑をかける to bother, to trouble
memo メモ note (written)
men 綿 cotton
mendô na 面倒な troublesome
menkyo 免許 permit, license
menkyoshô 免許証（運転） licence (for driving)
menrui 麺類 noodles
menyû メニュー menu

meron メロン melon
meshitsukai 召使 servant
mezameru 目覚める to wake up
mezurashii 珍しい rare (scarce)
mibôjin 未亡人 widow
miburi 身振り gesture
miburuisuru 身震いする to shiver
michi 道 road, street
michibiku 導く to lead, to guide
midori no 緑の green (adjective)
migaku 磨く to brush, to polish
migigawa 右側 right-hand side
migoto na 見事な great, impressive
migurushii 見苦しい ugly
miharu 見張る to watch over, to guard
mihon 見本 sample
mijikai 短い brief, short
mikake 見かけ appearance, looks
mikata 見方 viewpoint
mimi 耳 ear
minami 南 south
minamoto 源 source
minato 港 harbor, port
minzoku shûdan 民族集団 ethnic group
miru 観る to watch (show, movie)
miru 見る to watch, to look, to see
miryokuaru 魅力ある attractive
mise 店 shop, store
miseijuku no 未成熟の unripe
miseru 見せる to show
mitasu 満たす to fill
mite 見て look!
mitomeru 認める to recognize
mitsukeru 見つける to find
mitsumoru 見積もる to estimate
mitsurin 密林 jungle
mitsuyunyûsuru 密輸入する to smuggle
miyagemono みやげ物 souvenir
mizu 水 water
mizugi 水着 swimming costume, swimsuit
mizusashi 水差し jug, pitcher
mizushibuki 水しぶき splash
mizutama no 水玉の spotted (pattern)
mizuumi 湖 lake
mochiageru 持ち上げる（物を） to pick up, to lift (something)
mochidasu 持ち出す（話題を） to bring up (topic)
mochigome もち米 glutinous rice, sticky rice
mochiron もちろん certainly!, of course
modoru 戻る to return, to go back
moetsukita 燃え尽きた burned down
môfu 毛布 blanket
môhitotsu no もうひとつの another
moji 文字 character (written)
mokugekisha 目撃者 witness
mokugekisuru 目撃する to witness
mokuhyô 目標 goal
mokusei no 木製の wooden
mokuteki 目的 purpose
mokutekichi 目的地 destination
mokuyôbi 木曜日 Thursday
~mo mata ～もまた as well, too, also
momo もも thigh
~mo~mo~nai ～も～も～ない neither... nor
mômoku 盲目 blindness
mon 門 gate
mondai 問題 matter, issue, problem
mondainai 問題ない no problem
monitâ モニター（コンピューター） monitor (of computer)
mono 物 thing
moreguchi 漏れ口 leak
mori 森 forest

M

moshi もし if
môshikomu 申し込む to apply
moshimoshi もしもし hello (on phone)
mosuku モスク mosque
motâ モーター motor, engine
moto ni shita 基にした based on
motomeru 求める to seek
mottekuru 持ってくる to bring
mottomo 最も most (superlative)
mottomo hidoi 最もひどい worst
moyô 模様 pattern, design
moyô no aru 模様のある patterned
moyôshi 催し show (live performance)
muchi no 無知の ignorant
mueki na 無益な useless
mugon no 無言の silent
muimi na kotoba 無意味な言葉 nonsense
mukashi 昔 old times, past
mukashi no 昔の past, former
mukatsukuyô na むかつくような disgusting
muku 剥く to peel
mune 胸 chest (breast)
mura 村 village
murasaki no 紫の purple (adjective)
muryô de 無料で free of charge
musareta 蒸された steamed
museigen ni 無制限に free of restraints
mushisuru 無視する to ignore
musubu 結ぶ to tie
musuko 息子 son
musume 娘 daughter
muzukashii 難しい difficult
myanmâ ミャンマー Myanmar
myôji 苗字 surname

N

na 名（姓に対する名）given name
nabe 鍋 pan
nagai 長い（距離、時間）long (length, time)
nagaisu 長いす couch, sofa
nagasa 長さ length
nageru 投げる to throw
naibu 内部 inside
naifu ナイフ knife
nairon ナイロン nylon
nakaniwa 中庭 courtyard
naku 泣く to cry, to weep
nama no 生の raw, uncooked, rare
namae 名前 name
namayake no 生焼けの rare (half-cooked)
nameraka na なめらかな smooth, glassy
nameru 舐める to lick
nami 波 wave (in sea)
namida 涙 tears
nan no tame ni 何のために what for
nana 七 seven
nanajû 七十 seventy
nani 何 what
naniga okita 何が起きた what happened
nanika 何か anything, something
nanimo~nai 何も〜ない nothing
nanji 何時 what time
nanjûbaimo no 何十倍もの tens of, multiples of ten
nanpurâ ナンプラー fish sauce
nantô 南東 south-east
nansei 南西 south-west
naosu 直す to mend
narabu 並ぶ to line up
narasu 鳴らす（ベルを）to ring (bell)
narau 習う to learn

nareteiru 慣れている to be used to, to be accustomed
~nashi ni ～なしに without
nasu ナス aubergine, eggplant
natsu 夏 summer
naze なぜ why
nazenara なぜなら because
ne 根（植物）root (of plant)
nebanebashita ねばねばした sticky
nebumi o suru 値踏みをする to value
nedan 値段 price
neko 猫 cat
nekutai ネクタイ tie, necktie
nemaki 寝巻き nightclothes, nightdress
nemui 眠い sleepy
nemutte 眠って asleep
nenchô no 年長の elder
neru 寝る to go to bed, to sleep
nesoberu 寝そべる to lie down
nezumi ねずみ mouse, rat
~ni ～に on, at, in
~ni fureru ～に触れる to touch
~ni hairu ～に入る come in, enter
~ni hanshite ～に反して contrary to
~ni haru ～に貼る to stick to
~ni ichisuru ～に位置する to be located
~ni ittakoto ga aru ～に行ったことがある have been somewhere
~ni kakeru ～に掛ける to hang
~ni kanshite ～に関して concerning, regarding
~ni kuwaete ～に加えて in addition to
~ni kyômi ga aru ～に興味がある interested in
~nimo kakawarazu ～にもかかわらず in spite of
~ni naru ～になる to become
~ni notte ～に乗って on board
~ni shiraseru ～に知らせる to let someone know
~ni tsuite ～について about (regarding)
~ni tsuite hanasu ～について話す to talk about
~ni tsuite wasureru ～について忘れる to forget about
~ni tsuzuku ～に続く to follow along
~ni yoruto ～によると according to
~ni yotte ～によって（作者、芸術家） by (author, artist)
ni 二 two
nibai no 二倍の double
nicchû 日中 daytime
nichiyôbi 日曜日 Sunday
nigai 苦い bitter
nigatsu 二月 February
nigeru 逃げる to run away
nigiyaka na にぎやかな busy, lively (crowded), cheerful
nihon 日本 Japan
nihon(jin) no 日本（人）の Japanese
nijû 二十 twenty
nikki 日記 diary, journal
nikomi 煮込み soup (spicy stew)
nikudango 肉団子 meatball
ninjin 人参 carrot
ninki no aru 人気のある popular
ninmeisuru 任命する to appoint
ninniku にんにく garlic
nise no にせの false (imitation)
ninshinsuru 妊娠する to get pregnant
nintai no aru 忍耐のある patient (calm)
nishi 西 west

N

nita 煮た boiled
niwa 庭 garden, yard
niwatori 鶏 chicken, rooster
~no ～の of, from
~no aida ～の間（時間、年） in (time, years), during
~no aida ni ～の間に among, while, during, between
~no atode ～のあとで after
~no hô e ～の方へ toward
~no hôhô ～の方法 the way of
~no hôhô de ～の方法で by means of
~no jôtai ni aru ～の状態にある to be in a ~ situation/condition
~no kachi ga aru ～の価値がある to be worth
~no kawari ni ～の代わりに instead of
~no kekkatoshite ～の結果として as a result of
~no mae ni ～の前に before
~no mae ni ～の前に in front of
~no mukai ni ～の向かいに across from
~no naka ni ～の中に inside of, into
~no saichû ～の最中 in the middle of
~no shita ni ～の下に under
~no soba ni ～のそばに near
~no soto ni ～の外に outside of
~no ue ni ～の上に on, above
~no ushiro ni ～の後ろに behind
~no yô na ～のような like, as, such
~no yôni omowareru ～のように思われる to look, to seem, to appear
~no yôni mieru ～のように見える to look like
nô 脳 brain
noberu 述べる to express, to state, to mention
noboru 登る to go up, to climb
nodo のど throat
nodo no kawaita のどの渇いた thirsty
nokkusuru ノックする to knock
nokori 残り left, remaining, rest, remainder
nokorimono 残り物 remainder, leftover
nokoru 残る to stay, to remain
nomikomu 飲み込む to swallow
nomimono 飲み物 drink, beverage
nomu 飲む to drink
norimono 乗り物 vehicle
noriokureru 乗り遅れる（バス、飛行機） to miss (bus, flight)
noru 乗る（動物） to ride (animal)
noseru 乗せる（車） to give a lift
nôto ノート notebook
nozoite 除いて except
nozomi 望み desire, hope
nugu 脱ぐ（服） to take off (clothes)
nukumori ぬくもり warmth
nuno 布 cloth, fabric, textile
nureta 濡れた wet
nuu 縫う to sew
nyûjîlando ニュージーランド New Zealand
nyûjîlando(jin) no ニュージーランド（人）の New Zealander
nyûsu ニュース news
nyûyokusuru 入浴する to bathe, to take a bath

O

o 尾 tail
oba おば aunt
obake お化け ghost
obieta おびえた scared
oboeteiru 覚えている to remember
oboreru おぼれる to drown

ôbun オーブン oven
ochiru 落ちる to fall
odayaka na 穏やかな calm, mild (not severe)
odeko おでこ forehead
odori 踊り dance
odoroita 驚いた astonished, surprised
odorokubeki 驚くべき surprising
odoru 踊る to dance
ofisu オフィス office
ôfukukippu 往復キップ return ticket
ôgon 黄金 gold
oi 甥 nephew
oiharau 追い払う to chase away, to chase out
oikakeru 追いかける to chase
oishii おいしい delicious, tasty
oiteiku 置いていく leave behind on purpose
oji おじ uncle
oka 丘 hill
okashii おかしい funny
okidokei 置き時計 clock
ôkii 大きい big
ôkikunaru 大きくなる to grow larger
okiru 起きる to get up (from bed)
okiwasureru 置き忘れる to leave behind by accident, to lose, to mislay
okô お香 incense
okoru 起こる to happen, to occur
okoru 怒る to get angry
okosu 起こす to wake someone up
okotta 怒った cross, angry
oku 置く to place, to put
okure 遅れ delay
okureta 遅れた delayed
okurimono 贈り物 present (gift)
okurimono o suru 贈り物をする to present
okuru 送る to send
omedetô おめでとう congratulations!
omo ni 主に mainly
omosa 重さ weight
omocha おもちゃ toy
omoi 重い heavy
omoidasaseru 思い出させる to remind
omoshiroi おもしろい humorous
omou 思う to consider (to have an opinion), to think
onajitakasa no 同じ高さの of the same level (height)
onajiyô ni 同じように likewise
onaka ga ippai no お腹がいっぱいの full, eaten one's fill
ondo 温度 degrees (temperature)
onegaishimasu お願いします（何かを依頼する時）please (request for something)
oneuchi お値打ち good value
ongaku 音楽 music
oniai no お似合いの suitable, fitting, compatible
onna no ko 女の子 girl
onryô no aru 音量のある loud
onsen 温泉 hot spring
orenji オレンジ orange (citrus)
orenjiiro no オレンジ色の orange-colored (adjective)
oreru 折れる（骨など） to be broken, snapped (of bones, etc.)
orimono 織り物 weaving
oroka na 愚かな stupid
oru 織る to weave
oru 折る to fold
osaeru 抑える to restrain
ôsama 王様 king
oshieru 教える to teach, to tell, to let know
oshikumo 惜しくも regrettably
osoi 遅い late, slow

O

osokutomo 遅くとも at the latest
osoraku おそらく perhaps, probably
osore 恐れ fear
osu 押す to press, to push
ôsugiru 多過ぎる too much
ôsutoraria オーストラリア Australia
ôsutoraria(jin) no オーストラリア（人）の Australian
oto 音 sound, noise
ôtobai オートバイ motorcycle
otoko no hito 男の人 man
otoko no ko 男の子 boy
otôto 弟 younger brother
ototoi 一昨日 day before yesterday
otto 夫 husband
ôu 覆う to cover
owari 終わり end (finish)
owaru 終る to end
owatta 終った finished, gone, over
oyogu 泳ぐ to bathe, to swim
ôyoso おおよそ approximately, roughly
ôyoso no おおよその approximate, rough

P

pai パイ pie
painappuru パイナップル pineapple
pajama パジャマ pajamas, pyjamas
pan パン bread
panorama パノラマ panorama
pantsu パンツ（下着） shorts (underpants)
pantî パンティー panties
papaiya パパイヤ papaya
pâsento パーセント percent, percentage
pasupôto パスポート passport
pâtî パーティー party (event)
pechikôto ペチコート slip (petticoat, underskirt)
pêji 頁 page
pen ペン pen
penisu ペニス penis
penki ペンキ paint
penki o nuru ペンキを塗る（家、家具） paint, to (house, furniture)
petto ペット pet animal
pînattsu ピーナッツ peanut
pinku no ピンクの pink (adjective)
pittarishita ぴったりした tight-fitting
poketto ポケット pocket
ponpu ポンプ pump
puragu プラグ plug (electric)
puramu プラム plum
purasuchikku プラスチック plastic
pûru プール swimming pool

R

raichi ライチ lychee
raimu ライム lime, citrus
rainen 来年 next year
raishû 来週 next week
raitâ ライター lighter
rajio ラジオ radio
ramu ラム lamb
ranpu ランプ lamp
raosu ラオス Laos
raosu(jin) no ラオス（人）の Laotian
rasenjô no らせん状の spiral
rei 例 example
reigitadashii 礼儀正しい polite
reizôko 冷蔵庫 refrigerator
rekishi 歴史 history
remon レモン lemon (citrus)
remongurasu レモングラス（香草） lemongrass
reinen no 例年の annual
renketsusuru 連結する to connect together

renrakusuru 連絡する to contact, to get in touch with
renshûsuru 練習する to practise
repôtâ レポーター reporter
reshipi レシピ recipe
ressha de 列車で by rail
ressun レッスン lesson
resutoran レストラン restaurant
retsu 列 queue, line
retsu o tsukuru 列をつくる to queue, to line up
ribon リボン ribbon
rieki 利益 profit
rikaisuru 理解する to understand
rikonshita 離婚した divorced
rikonsuru 離婚する to divorce
rikugame 陸亀 tortoise (land)
ringo りんご apple
rinjin 隣人 neighbor
rinkaku 輪郭 border, edge
rishi 利子 interest
riyû 理由 reason
rô ロウ wax
rojji ロッジ lodge, small hotel
rôka 廊下 corridor
roku 六 six
rokugasuru 録画する to videotape
rokugatsu 六月 June
rokujû 六十 sixty
rôpu ロープ rope
rôsoku ろうそく candle
ruiji 類似 resemble
ruijin'en 類人猿 ape
ruijishita 類似した similar
rusubandenwa 留守番電話 answering machine, voicemail
ryô 量 amount
ryôgae 両替 exchange
ryôhô 両方 both
ryoken 旅券 passport
ryôkin 料金 fee, rate, tariff, fare
ryokô o suru 旅行をする to travel
ryokôannai 旅行案内 guidebook
ryokôsha 旅行者 traveler
ryôri 料理 cooking, cuisine, dish (particular food)
ryôrinin 料理人 cook (person)
ryôrisuru 料理する to cook
ryôshin 両親 parents
ryôshûsho 領収書 receipt
ryûchô na 流暢な fluent

S

sabaku 砂漠 desert (arid land)
sabishii 寂しい lonely
sâfin サーフィン surf
sagasu 探す to look for, to search for
sagi 詐欺 fraud
~sai ～歳 years old
sai 差異 difference (discrepancy in figures)
saifu 財布 wallet, purse
saigo 最後 last
saigo ni 最後に finally
saigo no 最後の final, last
saijitsu 祭日 holiday (festival)
sâ ikô さあ行こう come on, let's go
saikô no 最高の best
sain サイン signature
sainan 災難 disaster
saishô no 最小の smallest
saizu サイズ size
saka 坂 slope
sakaba 酒場 bar (serving drinks)
sakana 魚 fish
sakasama 逆さま upside down
sakasama no 逆さまの reversed, backwards
sake 酒 alcohol, liquor, sake
sakebu 叫ぶ to cry out, to shout, to yell

sakka 作家 writer
sakkâ サッカー soccer
saku 柵 fence
sakuhin 作品 composition, writings
sakunen 昨年 last year
sakuya 昨夜 last night
samasu 覚ます to awake, to wake up
samasu 冷ます to cool
samatageru 妨げる to disturb, to hinder, to prevent
same 鮫 shark
sameru 覚める to awake, to wake up
samui 寒い cold
san 三 three
sanchô 山頂 peak, summit
sandaru サンダル sandals
sangatsu 三月 March
sangoshô さんご礁 coral
sanjû 三十 thirty
sankaku 三角 triangle
sankasuru 参加する to go along, to join in, to participate
sanpo ni iku 散歩に行く to go for a walk
sara 皿 dish, platter, plate
sara ni 更に also
sararîman サラリーマン businessperson
saru 猿 monkey
sashikomi, 差込（電気）plug (electric)
sashô 査証 visa
sasou 誘う to invite (ask along)
sassoku 早速 immediately
satoru 悟る to realize, to be aware of
satô 砂糖 sugar
satôkibi サトウキビ sugarcane
sayamame さや豆 green beans
sayônara さようなら goodbye
sayônara to iu さようならと言う to say goodbye
sebone 背骨 spine
secchaku têpu 接着テープ adhesive tape
seibetsu 性別 sex, gender
seifu 政府 government
seiji 政治 politics
seijin no 成人の adult
seikaku 性格 character (personality)
seikaku na 正確な correct, exact
seikatsu 生活 life
seiketsu 清潔 cleanliness
seiki 世紀 century
seikô 性交 sex, sexual intercourse
seikô 成功 success
seikôsuru 成功する to succeed
seikyûsho 請求書 bill
seiri 生理 period (menstrual)
seiridansu 整理だんす chest (box)
seiryôinryôsui 清涼飲料 soft drink
seisansuru 生産する to produce
seishin no 精神の metal
seito 生徒 pupil, student
seitonsareta 整頓された orderly, organized, tidy
seitonsuru 整頓する to tidy up
seiyôjin 西洋人 westerner
seizôsuru 製造する to manufacture
sekai 世界 world
seki 咳き cough
sekikomu 咳きこむ to cough
sekinin 責任 responsibility
sekinin o motsu 責任を持つ to be responsible
sekken 石鹸 soap
sekkusu セックス sex, sexual intercourse
semai 狭い narrow
semeru 責める to blame
sen 千 thousand
sen 栓（風呂）plug (bath)

sen 線 line (mark)
senaka 背中 back (part of body)
senjôzai 洗浄剤 detergent
senkyo 選挙 election
senmonka 専門家 expert
senpûki 扇風機 fan (for cooling)
senro 線路 railroad, railway
sensei 先生 teacher
senshû 先週 last week
sensô 戦争 war
sensô o hajimeru 戦争を始める to start a war
sentaku 選択 choice
sentensu センテンス sentence
sentô 戦闘 battle
senzo 先祖 ancestor
serorî セロリー celery
setsumeisuru 説明する to explain
setsuzokusuru 接続する to join together
sewa o suru 世話をする to take care of, to look after
shakkin 借金 debt
shako 車庫 garage (for parking)
shakushi 杓子 ladle, dipper
shanpû シャンプー shampoo
sharin 車輪 wheel
shasen 車線（高速道路）lane (of a highway)
shashin 写真 photograph
shashin o toru 写真を撮る to photograph
shatsu シャツ shirt
shawâ シャワー shower (for washing)
shawâ o abiru シャワーを浴びる to take a shower
shi 市 city
shi 死 death
shiai 試合 match, game
shiawase 幸せ happiness
shibashiba しばしば often
shibô no ôi 脂肪の多い fatty, greasy
shichakusuru 試着する（服）to try on (clothes)
shichi 七 seven
shichigatsu 七月 July
shichû シチュー stew
shîdî シーディー CD
shîdî romu シーディーロム CD-ROM
shidôsha 指導者 leader
shigatsu 四月 April
shigeki no nai 刺激のない dull, monotonous
shigoto 仕事 job, work, occupation
shigoto o suru 仕事をする to work
shiharai 支払い payment
shihei 紙幣 note (currency)
shiiru 強いる to force, to compel
shijisuru 指示する to instruct, to tell to do something
shijisuru 支持する to back up
shikaku 資格 qualification
shikakui 四角い square (shape)
shikashi しかし however
shikashinagara しかしながら however, nevertheless
shiken 試験 exam, test
shikin 資金 funds, funding
shikirijô 仕切り状 invoice
shikke no aru 湿気のある damp, humid
shikô 思考 thoughts
shikyû 子宮 uterus
shima 島 island
shima no aru 縞のある striped
shimai 姉妹 sister
shimaru 閉まる to close
shimatta 閉まった shut, closed
shimi しみ stain
shimin 市民 citizen
~shinai ～しない no, not (with verbs and adjectives)
shinbun 新聞 newspaper

S

shinda 死んだ dead
shindai 寝台 bed
shingapôru シンガポール Singapore
shingurui 寝具類 bedding, bedclothes
shinjiru 信じる to believe
shinju 真珠 pearl
shinkôsuru 信仰する to worship
shinnen 信念 belief, faith
shinpaisuru 心配する to worry
shinraisuru 信頼する to trust
shinsei na 神聖な holy, sacred
shinseki 親戚 relatives
shinsen na 新鮮な fresh
shinshitsu 寝室 bedroom
shintô 神道 Shinto
shinu 死ぬ to die
shinwa 神話 myth
shinzô 心臓 heart
shio 塩 salt
shiokarai 塩辛い salty
shippai 失敗 failure
shippaisuru 失敗する to fail
shippo しっぽ tail
shiranai hito 知らない人 stranger
shiraseru 知らせる to inform
shiri 尻 bottom (buttocks)
shiriai 知り合い acquaintance
shiro 城 castle
shiro 白 white (noun)
shiru 知る to learn, to realize
shiryo no aru 思慮のある sensible
shisai 司祭 priest
shisan 資産 property, assets
shishoku o suru 試食をする to taste (sample)
shishû 刺繍 embroidery
shishunki no kodomo 思春期の子供（13～19歳） teenager
shishû no 刺繍の embroidered
shison 子孫 descendant
shissoku saseru 失速させる（車） to stall (car)
~shitai ～したい to want
~shitakoto ga aru ～したことがある have done something
~shitemoyoi ～してもよい can, may
shita 舌 tongue
shita e 下へ down, downward
shitagau 従う to obey
shitagi 下着 underwear
shîtsu シーツ bedsheet, sheet
shitsubôshita 失望した disappointed
shitsugyôchû no 失業中の unemployed
shitsumon 質問 question
shitsurei 失礼 impoliteness
shitsurei na 失礼な rude, impolite
shitsurei, nante osshaimashita ka 失礼、何ておっしゃいましたか pardon me, what did you say?
shitteiru 知っている to know
shitto 嫉妬 jealousy
shittobukai 嫉妬深い jealous
~shiyô ～しよう（提案）let's (suggestion)
shiyôdekiru 使用できる available
shizen 自然 nature
shizen no 自然の natural
shizuka na 静かな still, quiet
shô ショー show (live performance)
shôbai 商売 trade, business
shôben o suru 小便をする to urinate
shôchishita 承知した OK, all right!
shôdô o karitateru 衝動を駆り立てる urge, to push for
shôga 生姜 ginger
shôgai 障害 handicap, obstacle
shôgo 正午 midday, noon
shohôsen 処方箋 prescription
shôjiki na 正直な honest
shojisuru 所持する to own

shôkaisuru 紹介する to introduce someone
shokki o arau 食器を洗う wash the dishes
shokkidana 食器棚 cupboard
shôko 証拠 proof, evidence
shokubutsu 植物 plant
shokubutsuen 植物園 botanic gardens
shokugyô 職業 occupation, profession
shokuji 食事 meal
shokuniku 食肉 meat
shokuyôtori 食用鳥 poultry
shomei 署名 signature
shômei 照明 lighting
shômeisuru 証明する to prove
shomeisuru 署名する to sign
shôrai 将来 in future
shôron 小論 essay
shorui 書類 document
shôsan 賞賛 praise
shôsansuru 賞賛する admire, praise
shôsetsu 小説 novel
shôsho 証書 certificate
shôshô omachikudasai 少々お待ちください Please wait for a moment
shôtaisuru 招待する to invite (formally)
shotei no 所定の set
shôtotsu 衝突 collision
shôtotsusuru 衝突する to collide
shôtsu ショーツ shorts (short trousers)
shôyu しょう油 soy sauce (salty)
shoyûbutsu 所有物 belongings
shoyûken 所有権 the right of ownership
shoyûsuru 所有する to have, to own, to possess
shozokusuru 所属する to belong to
shû 週 **week**
shûchûsuru 集中する to concentrate
shuhin 主賓 guest of honor
shujin 主人 host
shûkan 習慣 custom, practice
shûkinsuru 集金する to collect money
shukôgei 手工芸 handicraft
shukuhakujo 宿泊所 accommodation
shukuhakushisetsu 宿泊施設 accommodations, facilities
shûkyô 宗教 religion
shûhen ni 周辺に around (surrounding)
shûmatsu 週末 weekend
shumi 趣味 hobby
shunkan 瞬間 moment (instant)
shuppansuru 出版する to publish
shuppatsu 出発 departure
shuppatsusuru 出発する to leave, to depart
shûrisuru 修理する to fix (repair)
shurui 種類 kind, type, sort
shushô 首相 prime minister
shussekisuru 出席する to attend
shuyô na 主要な main, most important
sô 層 layer
sobo 祖母 grandmother
sôchô ni 早朝に early in the morning
sôdai na 壮大な grand, great
sôdansuru 相談する to consult, to talk over with
sodateru 育てる（子供）to raise, to bring up
sodatsu 育つ（子供）to grow up (child)
sofâ ソファー couch, sofa
sofu 祖父 grandfather

S

JAPANESE—ENGLISH

S

sofubo 祖父母 grandparents
sôkan 壮観 spectacles
soketto ソケット（電気の）socket (electric)
sokkuri no そっくりの exactly like
soko de そこで there
sokonau 損なう to damage
soko ni そこに there
songai 損害 damage
sonkei 尊敬 respect
sonkeisuru 尊敬する to respect
sono aida ni その間に meanwhile
sono go その後 afterwards, later, after that
sono hito その人 that person
sono kekka その結果 therefore
sono ta no その他の the other
sono tôri その通り exactly! just so!
sono ue その上 besides, further, additional
sono yô ni そのように like that
sonzaisuru 存在する to exist
sora 空 sky
sore それ that one/matter
soredewa mata それではまた see you later!
sorenimo kakawarazu それにもかかわらず nevertheless
soreyue それゆえ therefore
soru 剃る to shave
sôshiki 葬式 funeral
sôshokuhin 装飾品 ornament
sosogu 注ぐ to pour
sôsu ソース sauce
sotogawa 外側 outside
sôzôsuru 想像する to imagine
su 酢 vinegar
su 巣 nest
subarashii すばらしい wonderful
~subeki de aru ～すべきである ought to, should
subesubeshita すべすべした smooth (of surfaces), glossy
subete 全て all
subete no 全ての every, whole, all of
subete no hito 全ての人 everybody, everyone
subete no mono 全ての物 everything
subete sorotta 全てそろった complete (whole)
sude ni すでに already
sugu ni すぐに in a moment, right now, immediately
sugusoba no すぐそばの close to, nearby
suicchi スイッチ switch
suigyû 水牛 buffalo (water buffalo)
suijun 水準 level (standard)
suika スイカ watermelon
suisokusuru 推測する to guess
suîtokôn スイートコーン sweet-corn
suiyôbi 水曜日 Wednesday
sûji 数字 figure, number
sukkari kawaku すっかり乾く（太陽で）to dry out (in the sun)
sukoshi 少し bit (slightly)
sukottorando スコットランド Scotland
sukottorando(jin) no スコットランド（人）の Scottish, Scots
sukunai 少ない few, little (not much)
sukunakunaru 少なくなる to lessen, to reduce
sukunakutomo 少なくとも at least
sukurîn スクリーン（コンピューター）screen (of computer)
sukâto スカート skirt
sumasu 済ます to finish off
sumâto na スマートな slender
sumi 墨 ink
sumimasen すみません excuse me!

sumu 住む to live (stay in a place)
suna 砂 sand
sunda 済んだ done (finished)
sunôendô スノーエンドウ snowpeas
sûpâmâketto スーパーマーケット supermarket
supîchi スピーチ speech
supîchi o suru スピーチをする to make a speech
supîdo スピード speed
suponji スポンジ sponge
supôtsu スポーツ sports
suppai すっぱい sour
supuringu スプリング spring (metal part)
supurê スプレー spray
sûpu スープ broth, soup
supûn スプーン spoon
suri すり pickpocket
surimu スリム slim
surippa スリッパ slippers
surippu スリップ slip (petticoat, underskirt)
suru する to do, to perform an action, to play
suru する to pickpocket
surudoi 鋭い sharp
~surukoto ga dekiru ～することができる to be able to
~surukoto o kyokasareru ～することを許可される to be allowed to
~surukoto o shôdakusuru ～することを承諾する to agree to do something
~surutame no ～するための for
~suru toki ～する時 when, at the time
~suru tsumori ～するつもり to (intend) mean
~suru yoyû ga aru ～する余裕がある to afford
susumeru 勧める to recommend
sutaffu スタッフ staff
sutanpu スタンプ stamp (ink)
suteki na 素敵な lovely, nice
suteru 捨てる to throw away, to throw out
sutoraiki o suru ストライキをする to go on strike
sûtsu スーツ business suit
sûtsukêsu スーツケース suitcase
suu 吸う to suck, to smoke
suwaru 座る to sit down, to sit
suzushii 涼しい cool

T

tabako タバコ cigarette
tabako o suu タバコをすう to smoke (tobacco)
tabaneteinai 束ねていない loose (not in packet)
tabemono 食べ物 food
tabemono o ataeru 食べ物を与える to feed
taberu 食べる to eat
tabi 旅 trip, journey
tabun 多分 perhaps
tachiagaru 立ち上がる to stand up
tadashii 正しい right, correct
tagarogu(jin) no タガログ（人）の Tagalog
tai タイ Thailand
tai(jin) no タイ（人）の Thai
taido 態度 attitude
taifû 台風 typhoon
taiju ga heru 体重が減る to lose weight
taijû ga fueru 体重が増える to gain weight
taikakusen ni 対角線に diagonally
taikakusen no 対角線の diagonal
taikôsha 対抗者 opponent

T

taikutsu na 退屈な dull (boring)
taikutsushita 退屈した bored
taiman na 怠慢な lazy
taipusuru タイプする to type
taira na 平らな level, plain (even, flat)
tairiku 大陸 continent
taishi 大使 ambassador
taishikan 大使館 embassy
taishitakotonai 大したことない minor (not important)
taisho 対処 dealing
taiyô 太陽 sun
taizai 滞在 visit
takai 高い high, tall
takameru 高める to lift, to raise
takarakuji 宝くじ lottery
takasa 高さ height
taki 滝 waterfall
takusan no たくさんの lots of, many, much
takushî タクシー taxi
takuwae 蓄え store, reserve
tamago 卵 egg
tamanegi 玉葱 onion
tamerau ためらう to hold back, to hesitate
tamesu 試す to test
tamotsu 保つ to keep, to save
tanbo 田んぼ rice fields
tane 種 seed
tani 谷 valley
tanjikan 短時間 short time, a moment
tanjôbi 誕生日 birthday, date of birth
tanjôbi omedetô 誕生日おめでとう happy birthday!
tan ni 単に merely
tanomu 頼む（非公式に） to request (informally)
tanoshimeru 楽しめる enjoyable
tanoshimi 楽しみ pleasure, delight
tanoshimu 楽しむ to enjoy oneself, to have fun
tanpan 短パン shorts (short trousers)
tansha 単車 motorcycle
taoru タオル towel
tashika ni 確かに indeed, surely
tashikameru 確かめる to check, to verify
tasseisuru 達成する to attain, to reach
tasukeru 助ける to assist, to help
tasukete 助けて help!
tatemono 建物 building
tateru 建てる to build
tatoeba 例えば such as, for example
tatsu 立つ to stand
tatta hitotsuno たった一つの sole, only
tatta ima たった今 just now
tatta no たったの just, only
tatta~dake たった〜だけ only
tazuneru 尋ねる to ask about, to enquire
tazuneru 訪ねる to go around, to visit, to stop by, to pay a visit
te 手 hand
tearai 手洗い toilet, restroom
têburukurosu テーブルクロス tablecloth
têburumatto テーブルマット tablemat
tegami 手紙 letter
tegoro na 手ごろな（値段） reasonable (price)
tehai 手配 arrangements, planning
teian 提案 suggestion
teiansuru 提案する to suggest
teido 程度 degree, level
teikyô 提供 offering

teikyôsuru 提供する to offer, to suggest
teiryûjo 停留所（バス、電車） stop (bus, train)
teiseisuru 訂正する to correct
teishutsu 提出 handing out, submission
teki 敵 enemy
tekisetsu na 適切な appropriate, fitting, suitable
tekubi 手首 wrist
ten 点 point, dot
tenimotsu 手荷物 baggage, luggage
ten'in 店員 sales assistant, shopkeeper
tenisu テニス tennis
tenji 展示 display
tenjisuru 展示する to display
tenjô 天井 ceiling
tenkeiteki na 典型的な typical
tenkensuru 点検する to inspect
tenki 天気 weather
tenpi 天火 oven
têpu no rokuon テープの録音 tape recording
terebi テレビ TV, television
tesûryô 手数料 fee
tetsu no 鉄の iron
tîshatsu ティーシャツ teeshirt
~to 〜と and, with
~to hanarete 〜と離れて apart from~
~to hikakusuru 〜と比較する compared with~
~to omowareru 〜と思われる to seem
~to onaji 〜と同じ same as~
~to~ryôhô 〜と〜両方 both…and
to 戸 door
tô 党（政治的な） party (political)
tô 塔 tower
toboshii 乏しい scarce
tobu 跳ぶ to jump
tôchaku 到着 arrival
tôchakusuru 到着する to arrive, to reach, to get to
tochi 土地 land
tochû de 途中で on the way
tôfu 豆腐 beancurd, tofu
tôgarashi 唐辛子 chilli pepper
tôgarashisôsu 唐辛子ソース chilli sauce
toho de 徒歩で on foot
tôhyôsuru 投票する to vote
toire トイレ toilet, restroom
tojiru 閉じる to shut
tokeisô no kajitsu トケイソウの果実 passionfruit
tokidoki 時々 from time to time, sometimes
tokoro de ところで by the way
tokoya 床屋 barber
toku ni 特に particularly, especially
tokubetsu na 特別な special
tokubetsu no 特別の extra
tokuchô 特徴 characteristics
tokei 時計 clock, watch
tôku e 遠くへ afar
tomato トマト tomato
tomatta 止まった off (turned off), stopped
tomeru 止める to stop, to halt
tomo ni 共に together
tomodachi 友達 friend
tomonau 伴う to involve, to escort
tômorokoshi トウモロコシ corn, grain
tonari ni 隣に next to
tora トラ tiger
toraeru 捕らえる to capture
torakku トラック truck
toranpu トランプ cards
tori 鳥 bird
torikesu 取り消す to cancel

T

tôrikosu 通り越す to pass, to go past
torinozoku 取り除く to rid, to get rid of
tôrinukete 通り抜けて through, past
tôrokusuru 登録する to register
toshi 都市 city
toshi 年 age, year
toshi no 都市の urban
toshitotta 年取った（人）old (of persons)
toshokan 図書館 library
totemo とても very
totemo chîsa na とても小さな tiny
totemo takusan no とてもたくさんの a large number of
totonoeru 整える to arrange
totte 取っ手 handle
tôtte 通って via
tsugi ni 次に next, secondly
tsugi no 次の next (in line, sequence), the following
tsuiyasu 費やす to spend
tsûjô no 通常の regular, normal
tsûka 通貨 currency
tsukaeru 仕える to serve
tsukaifurushita 使い古した（服、機械）worn out (clothes, machine)
tsukamaeru 捕まえる to catch
tsukamu つかむ to hold, to grasp
tsukarekitta 疲れ切った burned down, exhausted
tsukareta 疲れた weary, worn out, tired
tsukau 使う to use
tsukekuwawatta 付け加わった plus
tsukeru 点ける to switch on, to turn (something) on
tsuki 月 moon
tsukitôshita 突き通した pierced, penetrated
tsukue 机 table
tsukue o naraberu 机を並べる to lay the table
tsukuru 作る to create, to make
tsumaranai つまらない boring
tsumasaki つま先 toe
tsume 爪（手、足）nail (finger, toe)
tsumikomu 積み込む to load up
tsumini 積み荷 load
tsureai つれあい partner (spouse)
tsuru 釣る to fish
tsute つて contact, connection
tsutsumi 包み pack, wrap
tsûyakusha 通訳者 interpreter
tsuyoi 強い strong
tsuzuru 綴る to spell

U

uchiakeru 打ち明ける to admit, to confess
uchikatsu 打ち勝つ to overcome
uchimakasu 打ち負かす to beat (to defeat)
uchiwa うちわ fan (for cooling)
uchiyoseru nami 打ち寄せる波 surf
ude 腕 arm
udedokei 腕時計 watch (wristwatch)
udewa 腕輪 bracelet
ue no 上の top
ue no hô e 上のほうへ up, upward
ueru 植える to plant
ugoki 動き movement, motion
ugoku 動く to move
uketoru 受け取る to accept, to get, to receive
uma 馬 horse
umareru 生まれる to be born
umi 海 ocean, sea
umigame 海ガメ turtle (sea)
umu 産む to give birth

un 運 luck
un'eisuru 運営する to manage, to run
untensuru 運転する（車）to drive (a car)
uragaesu 裏返す over, to turn over
urareta 売られた sold
urayamashisa 羨ましさ envy
urayamashisô na 羨ましそうな envious
ureshiku omou うれしく思う to be glad
urikire 売り切れ sold out
urimono 売りもの for sale
uru 売る to sell
urusai うるさい noisy
ushi 牛 cow
ushinatta 失った lost (missing)
ushiro 後ろ back, rear, tail
ushiro e susumu 後ろへ進む to go backwards
ushiro kara tsuitekuru 後ろからついてくる to follow behind
ushiromuki ni 後ろ向きに backward
uso o tsuku 嘘をつく to lie, to tell a falsehood
uta 歌 song
utagau 疑う to doubt, to suspect
utau 歌う to sing
utsu 撃つ to shoot
utsu 打つ to strike, to hit
utsukushii 美しい beautiful
utsushi 写し copy
uttaeru 訴える to accuse, to sue
uwabaki 上履き slippers

W

wadai 話題 topic
wakai 若い young
wakamono 若者 youth (young person)
wakareta 分かれた separate
wakasa 若さ youth (state of being young)
wakemae 分け前 portion, share
wakeru 分ける to separate
wakimizu 湧き水 spring (of water)
wakkusu ワックス wax
wakuwakusaseru わくわくさせる exciting
wakuwakushita わくわくした excited
wan 湾 bay
wanpaku na 腕白な naughty
warau 笑う to laugh, to smile
wareware no 我々の our
waribiki 割引 discount
warui 悪い bad, wicked, wrong (morally)
warukunatte 悪くなって off (gone bad)
wasurerareta 忘れられた forgotten
wasureru 忘れる to forget
watashibune 渡し舟 ferry
watashi no 私の my, mine
watashi o 私を me
watashi wa 私は I
watashitachi o 私たちを us
watashitachi wa 私たちは we
watasu 渡す to hand over
wazuka わずか bit (part)
wazuka ni わずかに slightly
wazuka no わずかの a little, slight
webusaito ウェブサイト website
wêruzu ウェールズ Wales
wêruzu(jin) no ウェールズ(人)の Welsh

Y

yaburu 破る to tear, to rip
yagi 山羊 goat
yakareta 焼かれた baked, fried

Y

yakedo 火傷 burn (injury)
yakeru 焼ける to burn
yakigushi 焼き串 skewer
yakkyoku 薬局 drugstore, pharmacy
yaku 焼く to bake, to fry, to grill
yaku 約 about (approximately)
yakudatsu 役立つ to be useful
yakunin 役人（政府）officials (government)
yakusokusuru 約束する to promise
yakuwari 役割 role
yama 山 mountain
yameru やめる to stop, to cease, to quit
yamete やめて don't! stop it!
yane 屋根 roof
yasai 野菜 vegetable
yasashii やさしい gentle, kind
yaseta やせた（人）thin (of persons)
yashinau 養う to grow, to cultivate
yasui 安い cheap
yasumu 休む to rest, to relax
yasuuri 安売り sale (reduced prices)
yasuurisuru 安売りする to bargain
yatô 雇う to hire
yawarakai やわらかい soft
yoake 夜明け dawn
yobareteiru 呼ばれている to be called, named
yôbi 曜日 day of the week
yobidasu 呼び出す to call, to summon
yobôsesshu 予防接種 vaccination
yobun no 余分の extra
yôgosuru 擁護する） defend
yoi 良い well, good
yôi ga dekiteiru 用意ができている prepared, ready
yôisuru 用意する to arrange, to prepare
yoitabi o 良い旅を bon voyage!
yojinoboru よじ登る to climb onto
yokinsuru 預金する to deposit (put money in the bank)
yokisuru 予期する to expect
yokodaoshi ni suru 横倒しにする to lay sideways
yoko 横 side
yokogiru 横切る to cross, to go over
yokogitte 横切って across
yôkoso ようこそ welcome!
yoku dekimashita よくできました well done!
yokuaru よくある common, frequent
yoku hi no tôtta よく火の通った well-cooked, well-done
yokushitsu 浴室 bathroom
yoku~shitamonoda よく～したものだ used to do something
yôkyûsuru 要求する to demand
yômô 羊毛 wool
yomu 読む to read
yon 四 four
yonbun no ichi 四分の一 quarter
yonjû 四十 forty
yopparau 酔っ払う to get drunk
~yori ～より than
~yori mushiro ～よりむしろ rather than
~yori ôku ～より多く more than
~yori ue ni ～より上に above
yori sukunaku より少なく less (smaller amount) than
yori warui より悪い worse
yori yoi よりよい better
yôroppa ヨーロッパ Europe
yoru 夜 night
yoru ni 夜に at night
yoru no 夜の of the night
yoruosoku 夜遅く late at night
yôsai 要塞 fortress

yôshi 用紙 form (to fill out)
yosoou 装う to pretend
yotei 予定 program, schedule, plan
yowai 弱い weak
yoyaku 予約 reservation, booking
yoyakusuru 予約する to reserve (ask for in advance)
yubi 指 finger
yûbin 郵便 post, mail
yûbinbutsu 郵便物 mail, post
yûbinkyoku 郵便局 post office
yubiwa 指輪 ring (jewellery)
yûfuku na 裕福な well off, wealthy
yûga na 優雅な elegant
yûgata 夕方 evening
yûguredoki 夕暮れ時 dusk
yuiitsu no 唯一の single (only one)
yuka 床 floor
yukai na 愉快な amusing, comical
yuki 雪 snow
yuki ga furu 雪が降る to snow
yukkuri ゆっくり slowly
yûkô na 有効な valid, effective
yukuefumei 行方不明 missing (lost person)
yûkyû no 有給の paid
yume 夢 dream
yume o miru 夢を見る to dream
yûmei na 有名な famous
yûnô na 有能な capable
yunyû 輸入 to import
yunyûsuru 輸入する to import
yuri ugokasu 揺り動かす to swing
yurui ゆるい loose, not tight
yurusu 許す to forgive
yûshoku 夕食 dinner, evening meal
yûshôsha 優勝者 champion
yûshû na 優秀な excellent
yushutsu 輸出 export
yushutsusuru 輸出する to export
yûsô 郵送 mailing
yûzai 有罪 guilty (of a crime)

Z

zaiakukan o kanjiru 罪悪感を感じる to feel guilty
zairyô 材料 material, ingredient
zankoku na 残酷な cruel
zannen 残念 what a shame!
zannen da 残念だ what a pity!
zannen nagara 残念ながら unfortunately
zasshi 雑誌 magazine
zenbu de 全部で altogether, in total
zenkei 全景 panorama
zenmen 前面 front
zenpô ni 前方に forward, in front
zenshinsuru 前進する to advance, to go forward
zenshu no 全種の every kind of
zentaikara mite 全体から見て on the whole
zentai no 全体の entire
zero 零 zero
zô 象 elephant
zô 像 statue
zôge 象牙 ivory
zôka 増加 rise, increase
zubon ズボン pants, trousers
zuga 図画 drawing
zuibun ずいぶん quite (very)
zuii no 随意の optional
zukkîni ズッキーニ courgettes, zucchini
zungurishita ずんぐりした stout, chubby

English–Japanese

A

abdomen fukubu 腹部
able to ~surukoto ga dekiru 〜することができる
about (approximately) yaku 約, ôyoso おおよそ
about (regarding) ~ni tsuite 〜について
above ~yori ue ni 〜より上に
abroad ~gaikoku de 外国で
absent kesseki 欠席
accept, to uketoru 受け取る
accident jiko 事故
accidentally gûzen ni 偶然に
accommodation shukuhakujo 宿泊所
accompany, to dôhansuru 同伴する
according to ~ni yori 〜により
accuse, to uttaeru 訴える
ache itami 痛み
ache, to itamu 痛む
acquaintance shiriai 知り合い
acquainted, to be ~o shitteiru 〜を知っている
across yokogitte 横切って
across from ~no mukaini 〜の向かいに
act, to furumau 振る舞う
action kôdô 行動
activity katsudô 活動
actually jissai ni 実際に
add, to kuwaete 加えて
address jûsho 住所
admire, to shôsansuru 賞賛する
admit, to uchiakeru 打ち明ける
adult seijin no 成人の
advance, to (go forward) zenshinsuru 前進する
advance money (deposit) maebaraisuru 前払いする
advice jogen 助言
advise, to jogensuru 助言する
aeroplane hikôki 飛行機
affect, to eikyô o ataeru 影響を与える
affection aijô 愛情
afford, to ~suru yoyû ga aru 〜する余裕がある
afraid kowagatte 恐がって
after ~no atode 〜のあとで
afternoon (3 pm to dusk) gogo 午後（午後三時から夕暮れ）
afternoon (midday) shôgo 正午
afterwards (then) sonogo その後
again futatabi 再び
age toshi 年
ago mae ni 前に
agree, to dôisuru 同意する
agree to do something, to ~surukoto o shôdakusuru 〜することを承諾する
agreed! shôchishita 承知した
agreement dôi 同意
air kûki 空気
air conditioning eakon エアコン
airmail kôkûbin 航空便
airplane hikôki 飛行機
airport kûkô 空港
a little wazuka no わずかの
a lot takusan たくさん
alcohol (liquor) sake 酒
alike dôyô ni 同様に
alive ikite 生きて

A

ENGLISH—JAPANESE

all subete 全て
alley komichi 小道
allow, to kyokasuru 許可する
allowed to ~surukoto o kyokasareru ～することを許可される
almost hotondo ほとんど
alone hitori de ひとりで
already sude ni すでに
also sara ni 更に
altogether zenbu de 全部で
although keredomo けれども
always itsumo いつも
ambassador taishi 大使
ambience fun'iki 雰囲気
America amerika アメリカ
American amerika(jin) no アメリカ（人）の
among ~no naka ni ～の中に
amount ryô 量
ancestor senzo 先祖
ancient kodai no 古代の
and ~to ～と, ~oyobi~ ～及び～
anger ikari 怒かり
angry okkotta 怒った
animal dôbutsu 動物
ankle kurubushi くるぶし
annoyed meiwakushita 迷惑した
another (different) betsu no 別の
another (same again) môhitotsu no もうひとつの
annual reinen no 例年の
answer (spoken) henji 返事
answer (written) henshin 返信
answer, to (spoken) henji o suru 返事をする
answer, to (written) henshinsuru 返信する
answer the phone, to denwa ni deru 電話にでる
answering machine rusubandenwa 留守番電話
antiques kottôhin 骨董品
anus kômon 肛門
anybody, anyone dareka だれか
anything nanika 何か
anywhere dokoka ni どこかに
ape ruijin'en 類人猿
apart hanarete 離れて
apartment apâto アパート
apologize, to ayamaru 謝る
apparently dôyara~rashii どうやら～らしい
appear, to arawareru 現れる
appearance mikake 見かけ
apple ringo りんご
appliance denki kiki 電気機器
apply, to môshikomu 申し込む
appointment ninmei 任命
approach, to (in space) chikazuku 近づく（空間）
approach, to (in time) chikazuku 近づく（時間）
appropriate tekisetsu na 適切な
approximately ôyoso おおよそ
April shigatsu 四月
architecture kenchiku 建築
area chiiki 地域
argue, to gironsuru 議論する
argument giron 議論
arm ude 腕, buki 武器
armchair hijikakeisu ひじ掛け椅子
army guntai 軍隊
around (approximately) ôyoso おおよそ
around (nearby) chikaku de 近くで
around (surrounding) shûhen ni 周辺に
arrange, to totonoeru 整える, yôisuru 用意する
arrangements (planning) tehai 手配
arrival tôchaku 到着
arrive, to tôchakusuru 到着する
art geijutsu 芸術
article (in newspaper) kiji 記事

artificial jinkô no 人工の
artist geijutsuka 芸術家
as well ~mo mata 〜もまた
ashamed hajite 恥じて
Asia ajia アジア
ask about, to tazuneru 尋ねる
ask for, to iraisuru 依頼する
asleep nemutte 眠って
assemble, to (gather) atsumeru 集める
assemble, to (assemble) kumiawaseru 組み合わせる
assist, to tasukeru 助ける
assistance enjo 援助
astonished odoroita 驚いた
at ~de 〜で, ~ni 〜に
at home ie de 家で
at night yoru ni 夜に
at once sugu ni すぐに
atmosphere fun'iki 雰囲気
attack (in war) kôgeki 攻撃（戦争）
attack (with words) hinan 非難（言葉で）
attain, to tasseisuru 達成する
attempt kokoromi 試み
attempt, to kokoromiru 試みる
attend, to shussekisuru 出席する
at the latest osokutomo 遅くとも
attitude taido 態度
attractive miryokuaru 魅力ある
aubergine nasu ナス
auction, to kyôbai ni kakeru 競売にかける
auctioned off kyôbai ni kakerareta 競売にかけられた
August hachigatsu 八月
aunt oba おば
Australia ôsutoraria オーストラリア
Australian ôsutoraria(jin) no オーストラリア（人）の
authority (person in charge) ken'i 権威
authority (power) kenryokusha 権力者
automobile jidôsha 自動車
autumn aki 秋
available shiyôdekiru 使用できる
available, to make kanô ni suru 可能にする
average (numbers) heikin 平均
average (so-so, just okay) hitona-mi 人並み
awake me ga samete 目が覚めて
awake, to sameru 覚める
awaken, to okosu 起こす
aware kizuiteiru 気づいている
aware: be aware of, to satoru 悟る
awareness jikaku 自覚

B

baby akachan 赤ちゃん
back (part of body) senaka 背中
back (rear) ushiro 後ろ
back, to go modoru 戻る
back up, to shijisuru 支持する
backward ushiromuki ni 後ろ向きに
bad warui 悪い
bad luck fuun 不運
bag kaban 鞄
baggage tenimotsu 手荷物
bake, to yaku 焼く
baked yakareta 焼かれた
bald hageta はげた
ball bôru ボール
ballpoint pen bôrupen ボールペン
banana banana バナナ
bandage hôtai 包帯
bank (finance) ginkô 銀行
bank (of river) dote 土手
banquet enkai 宴会
bar (blocking way) kôshi 格子
bar (serving drinks) bâ バー, sakaba 酒場

barber tokoya 床屋
barely karôjite かろうじて
bargain yasuuri 安売り
barren fumô no 不毛の
base (foundation) kiso 基礎
based on ~o moto ni shita 〜を基にした
basic kihon 基本
basis dodai 土台
basket kago かご
basketball basukettobôru バスケットボール
bath furo 風呂
bathe, to (swim) oyogu 泳ぐ
bathe: to take a bath nyûyokusuru 入浴する
bathrobe basurôbu バスローブ、yukata 浴衣
bathroom yokushitsu 浴室
battle sentô 戦闘
bay wan 湾
be, to (exist) sonzaisuru 存在する
be able to ~dekiru 〜できる
beach bîchi ビーチ, hamabe 浜辺
bean mame 豆
beancurd tôfu 豆腐
beard agohige あごひげ
beat, to (to defeat) uchimakasu 打ち負かす
beat, to (to strike) hageshiku utsu 激しく打つ
beautiful kirei na きれいな, utsukushii 美しい
because nazenara なぜなら
become, to ~ni naru 〜になる
become visible, to arawareru 現れる
bed beddo ベッド, shindai 寝台
bedclothes, bedding shingurui 寝具類
bedroom shinshitsu 寝室
bedsheet shîtsu シーツ
beef gyûniku 牛肉
beer bîru ビール
before (in front of) ~no maeni 〜の前に
before (in time) izen ni 以前に
beforehand arakajime あらかじめ
begin, to hajimeru 始める
beginning hajime 始め
behave, to furumau 振る舞う
behind ~no ushiro ni 〜の後ろに
belief (faith) shinnen 信念
believe, to shinjiru 信じる
belly hara 腹
belongings shoyûbutsu 所有物
belong to, to shozokusuru 所属する
below (downstairs) kaika ni 階下に
belt beruto ベルト
beside ~no toko ni 〜の横に
besides sonoue その上
best saikô no 最高の
best wishes gotakô o inorimasu ご多幸を祈ります
better yoriyoi よりよい
better (improve) genki ni naru 元気になる, yokunaru よくなる
between ~no aida ni 〜の間に
bicycle jitensha 自転車
big ôkii 大きい
bill seikyûsho 請求書
billion jûoku 十億
bird tori 鳥
birth, to give umu 産む
birthday tanjôbi 誕生日
biscuit (cookie) bisuketto ビスケット, kukkî クッキー
biscuit (cracker) kurakkâ クラッカー
bit (part) wazuka わずか
bit (slightly) sukoshi 少し
bite, to kamu 噛む
bitter nigai 苦い
black kuroi 黒い
black beans kuromame 黒豆

blame, to semeru 責める
bland onwa na 温和な
blanket môfu 毛布
blind mômoku no 盲目の
blood chi 血
blouse burausu ブラウス
blue aoi 青い
board, to (bus, train) jôshasuru 乗車する（バス、電車）
boat bôto ボート, kobune 小船
body karada 体
boil, to futtôsuru 沸騰する
boiled nita 煮た
bon voyage! Yoitabi o 良い旅を
bone hone 骨
book hon 本
border kyôkaisen 境界線
border (between countries) kokkyô 国境
border (edge) rinkaku 輪郭
bored taikutsushita 退屈した
boring tsumaranai つまらない
born, to be umareru 生まれる
borrow, to kariru 借りる
boss jôshi 上司
botanic garden shokubutsuen 植物園
both ryôhô 両方
both ... and ~to~ryôhô ～と～両方
bother, to jamasuru 邪魔する
bother meiwaku 迷惑
bottle bin 瓶
bottom (base) kontê 根底
bottom (buttocks) shiri 尻
boundary kyôkaisen 境界線
bowl donburi どんぶり
box hako 箱
box (cardboard) danbôrubako 段ボール箱
boy otoko no ko 男の子
boyfriend kareshi 彼氏
bra burajâ ブラジャー
bracelet udewa 腕輪
brain nô 脳
brain (mind) chiryoku 知力
brake burêki ブレーキ
brake, to burêki o kakeru ブレーキをかける
branch eda 枝
brave (daring) isamashii 勇ましい
bread pan パン
break, to konagona ni suru 粉々にする
break apart, to barabara ni suru ばらばらにする
break down, to (car, machine) koshôsuru 故障する
breakfast chôshoku 朝食
breakfast, to eat chôshoku o toru 朝食をとる
breasts mune 胸
bride hanayome 花嫁
bridegroom hanamuko 花婿
bridge hashi 橋
brief mijikai 短い
briefcase burîfukêsu ブリーフケース
briefs burîfu ブリーフ（下着）
bright akarui 明るい
bring, to mottekuru 持ってくる
bring up, to (children) sodateru 育てる（子供を）
bring up, to (topic) mochidasu 持ち出す（話題を）
British eikoku(jin) no 英国（人）の
broad (spacious) hiroi 広い
broadcast hôsô 放送
broadcast, to hôsôsuru 放送する
broccoli burokkorî ブロッコリー
broken (does not work) kowareta 壊れた
broken (of bones, etc.) oreta 折れた（骨など）
broken (shattered) konagonani kowareta 粉々に壊れた

B

ENGLISH–JAPANESE

broken off ~kara hazureta ～からはずれた
bronze dô 銅
broom hôki ほうき
broth sûpu スープ
brother (older) ani 兄
brother (younger) otôto 弟
brother-in-law (older sister's husband or wife's older brother) gikei 義兄
brother-in-law (younger sister's husband or wife's younger brother) gitei 義弟
brown chairoi 茶色い
bruise aza あざ
brush burashi ブラシ, hake はけ
brush, to migaku 磨く
bucket baketsu バケツ
Buddhism bukkyô 仏教
Buddhist bukkyôto 仏教徒
buffalo (water buffalo) baffarô バッファロー, suigyû 水牛
build, to tateru 建てる
building tatemono 建物
burn (injury) yakedo 火傷
burn, to yakeru 焼ける
burned down/out moetsukita 燃え尽きた, tsukarekitta 疲れ切った
Burma biruma ビルマ
Burmese biruma(jin) no ビルマ（人）の
bus basu バス
bus station basutei バス停
business shôbai 商売
businessperson jitsugyôka 実業家
busy (crowded) nigiyaka na にぎやかな
busy (doing something) isogashii 忙しい
busy (telephone) hanashichû 話し中（電話）
but demo でも
butter batâ バター
butterfly chôchô 蝶々
buttocks shiri 尻
buy, to kau 買う
by (author, artist) ~ni yotte ～によって（作者、芸術家）
by means of ~no hôhô de ～の方法で
by the way tokorode ところで

C

cabbage kyabetsu キャベツ
cabbage, Chinese hakusai 白菜
cake (pastry) kêki ケーキ, pai パイ
calculate, to keisansuru 計算する
calculator keisanki 計算機
call, to yobidasu 呼び出す
call on the telephone, to denwa o suru 電話をする
called yobareteiru 呼ばれている
calm odayaka na 穏やかな
Cambodia kanbojia カンボジア
Cambodian kanbojia(jin) no カンボジア（人）の
camera kamera カメラ
can ~dekiru ～できる
can (may) ~shitemoyoi ～してもよい
can (tin) kan 缶
cancel, to torikesu 取り消す
candle rôsoku ろうそく
candy ame 飴
capable of yûnô na 有能な
capture, to toraeru 捕らえる
car jidôsha 自動車
cardboard bôrugami ボール紙
cards (game) toranpu トランプ
care for, to konomu 好む
care of, to take sewa o suru 世話をする
careful! ki o tsukete 気をつけて
carpet jûtan 絨毯

carrot ninjin 人参
carry, to hakobu 運ぶ
cart (horsecart) basha 馬車
cart (pushcart) kâto カート(手押し)
carve, to horu 彫る
carving chôkoku 彫刻
cash genkin 現金
cash a check, to kogitte o kankinsuru 小切手を換金する
cassette kasetto カセット
cat neko 猫
catch, to tsukamaeru 捕まえる
cauliflower karifurawâ カリフラワー
cause gen'in 原因
cautious chûi bukai 注意深い
cave horaana 洞穴
CD shîdî シーディー
CD-ROM shîdî romu シーディーロム
ceiling tenjô 天井
celebrate, to iwau 祝う
celery serorî セロリー
cell phone keitai denwa 携帯電話
center (of city) hankagai 繁華街(町の)
center chûshin 中心
central chûshin no 中心の
century seeki 世紀
ceremony gishiki 儀式
certain tashika na 確かな
certainly! mochiron もちろん
certificate shôsho 証書
chair isu 椅子
challenge chôsen 挑戦
champion yûshôsha 優勝者
chance kikai 機会
chance, by gûzen ni 偶然に
change kozeni 小銭
change, to (clothes) kigaeru 着替える
change, to (conditions, situations) kawaru 変わる(状況が)
change, to (money) kankinsuru 換金する
change one's mind, to kaeru 変える
character (personality) seikaku 性格
character (written) moji 文字
characteristic dokutoku no 独特の
chase, to oikakeru 追いかける
chase away/out oiharau 追い払う
cheap yasui 安い
cheat peten ぺてん
cheat, to damasu だます
cheating (in a test/exam) kanningu カンニング
check, to tashikameru 確かめる
checked (pattern) chekku チェック
cheek hô 頬
cheers! kanpai 乾杯
cheese chîzu チーズ
chess chesu チェス
chest (box) seiridansu 整理だんす
chest (breast) mune 胸
chew, to kamu 噛む
chicken niwatori 鶏
child (offspring) kodomo 子供(子孫)
child (young person) kodomo 子供(若い人一般)
chilled hiyasareta 冷やされた
chilli pepper tôgarashi 唐辛子
chilli sauce tôgarashisôsu 唐辛子ソース, chiri sôsu チリソース
chin ago あご
China chûgoku 中国
Chinese chûgoku(jin) no 中国(人)の
chocolate chokorêto チョコレート
choice sentaku 選択
choose, to erabu 選ぶ
chopsticks hashi 箸
Christian kirisutokyô(to) no キリスト教(徒)の
Christianity kirisutokyô キリスト教
church kyôkai 教会

cigar hamaki 葉巻
cigarette tabako タバコ
cilantro koriandâ コリアンダー（香草）
cinema eigakan 映画館
circle en 円, maru 丸
citizen shimin 市民
citrus kankitsurui かんきつ類
city toshi 都市, machi 町, shi 市
class (category) bumon 部門
classes (at university) kurasu クラス（大学の）, jugyo 授業
clean kirei na きれいな
clean, to kirei ni suru きれいにする
cleanliness seiketsu 清潔
clear (of weather) hareta 晴れた（天気）
clever kashikoi かしこい
climate kikô 気候
climb onto, to yojinoboru よじ登る
climb up, to (hills, mountains) noboru 登る（丘、山）
clock okidokei 置き時計
close, to shimaru 閉まる
close to sugusoba no すぐそばの
close together kitsui きつい
closed (door) shimatta 閉まった（ドア）
closed (road) heisa 閉鎖（道）
closed (shop) heiten 閉店（店）
cloth nuno 布
clothes, clothing fuku 服
cloudy (overcast) kumotta 曇った
clove cigarette chôjitabako 丁子タバコ
cloves chôji 丁子
co-worker dôryô 同僚
coat (jacket) jaketto ジャケット, uwagi 上着
coat (overcoat) kôto コート, gaitô 外套
coconut kokonattsu ココナッツ
coffee kôhî コーヒー
coin kôka 硬貨
cold samui 寒い
cold (flu) kaze 風邪
colleague dôryô 同僚
collect money, to shûkinsuru 集金する
collide, to shôtotsusuru 衝突する
collision shôtotsu 衝突
color iro 色
comb kushi 櫛
come, to kuru 来る
come back fukki 復帰
come in, to ~ni hairu ～に入る
come on sâ ikô さあ行こう
comfortable kokochi yoi 心地良い
command (order) meirei 命令
command, to meireisuru 命令する
common yokuaru よくある
company kaisha 会社, kigyô 企業
compare, to hikakusuru 比較する
compared with ~to hikakushite ～と比較して
compel, to shiiru 強いる
compete, to kyôsôsuru 競争する
competition kyôsô 競争
complain, to fuhei o kobosu 不平をこぼす
complaint fuhei 不平, kujô 苦情
complete (finished) kanseishita 完成した
complete (thorough) kanpeki na 完璧な
complete (whole) subete sorotta 全てそろった
complete, to kanzen ni suru 完全にする
completely kanzen ni 完全に
complicated fukuzatsu na 複雑な
compose, to (letters, books, music) kaku 書く（手紙、本、曲）
composition sakuhin 作品

compulsory hissu no 必須の, gimuteki na 義務的な
computer konpyûtâ コンピューター
concentrate, to shûchûsuru 集中する
concerning ~ni kanshite ～に関して
condition (pre-condition) jôken 条件
condition (status) jôkyô 状況
confectionery kashi 菓子
confess uchiakeru 打ち明ける
confidence jishin 自信
confidence, to have jishin o motsu 自信を持つ
Confucianism jukyô 儒教
confuse, to konwakusaseru 困惑させる
confused (in a mess) konranshita 混乱した
confused (mentally) konwakushita 困惑した
confusing magirawashii 紛らわしい
congratulations! omedetô おめでとう
connect together, to renketsusuru 連結する
conscious of, to be jikakusuru 自覚する
consider, to (to have an opinion) omou 思う
consider, to (to think over) kôryosuru 考慮する
consult, to sôdansuru 相談する
contact, connection kone コネ, tsute つて
contact, to renrakusuru 連絡する
continent tairiku 大陸
continue, to keizokusuru 継続する
convenient benri na 便利な
conversation kaiwa 会話
cook (person) kokku コック, ryôrinin 料理人
cook, to ryôrisuru 料理する
cooked chôrisareta 調理された
cooker (stove) konro コンロ
cookie (sweet biscuit) kukkî クッキー, bisuketto ビスケット
cooking ryôri 料理
cool suzushii 涼しい
cool, to samasu 冷ます
copper dô 銅
copy utsushi 写し
coral sangoshô さんご礁
coriander koriandâ コリアンダー（香草）
corn (grain) tômorokoshi トウモロコシ
corner kado 角
correct seikaku na 正確な
correct, to teiseisuru 訂正する
correspond, to (write letters) buntsûsuru 文通する
corridor rôka 廊下
cost (expense) hiyô 費用
cost (price) kakaku 価格
cotton men 綿
couch sofâ ソファー, nagaisu 長いす
cough seki 咳き
cough, to sekikomu 咳きこむ
could hyottoshitara ~kamoshirenai ひょっとしたら～かもしれない
count, to kazoeru 数える
counter (for paying, buying tickets) kauntâ カウンター, kanjôdai 勘定台
country (nation) kokka 国家
country (rural area) inaka 田舎
courgettes zukkîni ズッキーニ
courtyard nakaniwa 中庭
cover, to ôu 覆う
cow ushi 牛
crab kani 蟹
cracked kudaketa 砕けた

cracker (salty biscuit) kurakkâ クラッカー
crafts kôgei 工芸
craftsperson kôgeika 工芸家
crate konpôbako 梱包箱
crazy kurutta 狂った
create, to tsukuru 作る
criminal hanzaisha 犯罪者
cross (angry) okotta 怒った
cross, to (go over) yokogiru 横切る
crowded konzatsushita 混雑した
cruel zankoku na 残酷な
cry, to naku 泣く
cry out, to sakebu 叫ぶ
cucumber kyuuri キュウリ
cuisine (style of cooking) ryôri 料理
culture bunka 文化
cup koppu コップ, chawan 茶わん
cupboard shokkidana 食器棚, todana 戸棚
cure (medical) chiryô 治療（医療）
cured hozonsareta 保存された
currency tsûka 通貨
curtain kâten カーテン
custom shûkan 習慣, dentô 伝統
cut (slice) kireme 切れめ
cut, to kiru 切る
cute (appealing) kawaii かわいい

D

daily mainichi no 毎日の
damage songai 損害
damage, to ~o sokonau ～を損なう
damp shikke no aru 湿気のある
dance odori 踊り
dance, to odoru 踊る
danger kiken 危険
dangerous kiken na 危険な
dark kurai 暗い
date (of the month) hizuke 日付
date of birth tanjôbi 誕生日
daughter musume 娘
daughter-in-law girino musume 義理の娘
dawn yoake 夜明け
day hi 日
day after tomorrow asatte 明後日
day before yesterday ototoi 一昨日
day of the week yôbi 曜日
day off kyûjitu 休日
daydream, to kûsôsuru 空想する
dead shinda 死んだ
deaf chôkakushôgai no aru 聴覚障害のある
death shi 死
debt shakkin 借金
deceive, to damasu だます
December jûnigatsu 十二月
decide, to kimeru 決める
decision kesshin 決心
decline, to (get less) kakôsuru 下降する
decline, to (refuse) kotowaru 断る
decorate, to kazaru 飾る
decrease, to heru 減る
deep fukai 深い
defeat, to uchimakasu 打ち負かす
defecate, to kiyomeru 清める, haibensuru 排便する
defect ketten 欠点
defend, to (in war) bôgyosuru 防御する（戦争）
defend, to (with words) yôgosuru 擁護する（言葉）
definite kakuteishita 確定した
degree (level) teido 程度
degrees (temperature) ondo 温度
delay okure 遅れ
delayed okureta 遅れた
delicious oishii おいしい
deliver, to haitatsusuru 配達する
demand, to yôkyûsuru 要求する
depart, to shuppatsusuru 出発する

department bu 部, ka 課
department store hyakkaten 百貨店, depâto デパート
departure shuppatsu 出発
depend on, to izonsuru 依存する
deposit, to (leave behind with someone) azukeru 預ける
deposit, to (put money in the bank) yokinsuru 預金する
descendant shison 子孫
describe, to byôshasuru 描写する
desert (arid land) sabaku 砂漠
desert, to (abandon) hôkisuru 放棄する
desire kibô 希望, ganbô 願望
desire, to nozomu 望む
desk desuku デスク, benkyôzukue 勉強机
dessert dezâto デザート
destination mokutekichi 目的地
destroy, to hakaisuru 破壊する
destroyed hakaisareta 破壊された
detergent senjôzai 洗浄剤
determined dankotoshita 断固とした
develop, to (film) genzôsuru 現像する
develop, to (happen) hattensuru 発展する
development hatten 発展, kaihatsu 開発
diagonal taikakusen no 対角線の
diagonally taikakusen ni 対角線に
dial, to (telephone) denwa o kakeru 電話をかける
dialect hôgen 方言
diamond daiyamondo ダイヤモンド
diary nikki 日記
dictionary jisho 辞書
die, to shinu 死ぬ
difference (discrepancy in figures) sai 差異
difference (in quality) sôi 相違
different (other) hoka no ほかの
difficult muzukashii 難しい
dinner yûshoku 夕食
dinner, to eat yûshoku o toru 夕食をとる
dipper hishaku ひしゃく
direction hôkô 方向
director (of company) jûyaku 重役（会社の）
dirty kitanai 汚い
disappointed shitsubôshita 失望した
disaster sainan 災難
discount waribiki 割引
discover, to hakkensuru 発見する
discuss, to gironsuru 議論する
discussion giron 議論
disease byôki 病気
disgusting mukatsukuyô na むかつくような
dish sara 皿
dish (particular food) ryôri 料理
diskette furoppîdisuku フロッピーディスク
dislike, to konomanai 好まない, kirau 嫌う
display tenji 展示
display, to tenjisuru 展示する
distance kyori 距離
disturb, to samatageru 妨げる
disturbance bôgai 妨害
divide, to bunkatsusuru 分割する
divided by ~de warareta ～で割られた
divorce, to rikonsuru 離婚する
divorced rikonshita 離婚した
do, to (perform an action) ~suru ～する
do one's best besuto o tsukusu ベストを尽くす
doctor isha 医者

document shorui 書類
do(es) not work (spoiled) kowareta 壊れた
dog inu 犬
done (cooked) yoku hi no tôtta よく火の通った
done (finished) sunda 済んだ
don't! shite wa dame してはだめ
don't mention it! dôitashimashite どういたしまして
door to 戸, doa ドア
double nibai no 二倍の
doubt, to utagau 疑う
down, downward shita e 下へ
downstairs kaika e 階下へ
downtown hankagai 繁華街
dozen dâsu ダース
draw, to hiku 引く
drawer hikidashi 引き出し
drawing zuga 図画
dream yume 夢
dream, to yume o miru 夢を見る
dress doresu ドレス
dressed, to get kiru 着る
dressing gown gaun ガウン
drink nomimono 飲み物
drink, to nomu 飲む
drive, to (a car) untensuru 運転する（車）
drought kanbatsu 干ばつ
drown, to oboreru おぼれる
drug (medicine) kusuri 薬
drug (narcotic) mayaku 麻薬
drugstore yakkyoku 薬局
drunk yopparatta 酔っ払った
dry kawaita 乾いた
dry (weather) kansôshita 乾燥した（天気）
dry, to kawakasu 乾かす
dry out (in the sun) sukkari kawaku すっかり乾く（太陽で）
duck ahiru アヒル
dull (boring) taikutsu na 退屈な
dull (weather) don'yorishita (tenki) どんよりした（天気）
dumpling dango 団子
durian dorian ドリアン
during ~no aida ni ～の間に
dusk yûgure doki 夕暮れ時
dust hokori 埃
duty (import tax) kanzei 関税
duty (responsibility) gimu 義務
DVD dîbuidî ディーブイディー

E

each ~goto ni ～毎に
ear mimi 耳
earrings iyaringu イアリング
earlier maemotte 前もって
early hayai 早い
early in the morning sôchô ni 早朝に
earn, to eru 得る
earth dojô 土壌
Earth chikyû 地球
earthquake jishin 地震
east higashi 東
easy kantan na 簡単な
eat, to taberu 食べる
economical keizaiteki na 経済的な
economy keizai 経済
edge hashi 端
educate, to kyôikusuru 教育する
education kyôiku 教育
effect eikyô 影響
effort doryoku 努力
effort: to make an effort doryokusuru 努力する
egg tamago 卵
eggplant nasu ナス
eight hachi 八
eighteen jûhachi 十八
eighty hachijû 八十

either dochiraka ippô no どちらか一方の
elbow hiji ひじ
elder nenchô no 年長の
election senkyo 選挙
electric denki no 電気の
electrical denki kiki 電気機器
electricity denki 電気
electronic denshi no 電子的の
elegant yûga na 優雅な
elephant zô 象
elevator erebêtâ エレベーター
eleven jûichi 十一
else: anything else sonota no その他の
else: or else ~de nakereba ～でなければ
email (message) denshi mêru 電子メール（メッセージ）
email (system) denshi mêru 電子メール（システム）
email, to denshi mêru o okuru 電子メールを送る
email address denshi mêru adoresu 電子メールアドレス
embarrassed batsu no warui ばつの悪い
embarrassing hazukashii 恥ずかしい
embassy taishikan 大使館
embrace, to idaku 抱く
embroidered shishû no 刺繍の
embroidery shishû 刺繍
emergency kinkyûjitai 緊急事態
emotion kanjô 感情
empty kara no 空の
end (finish) owari 終わり
end (tip) hashi 端
end, to owaru 終る
enemy teki 敵
energy katsuryoku 活力
engaged (telephone) hanashichû 話し中
engaged (to be married) konyakuchû no 婚約中の
engine enjin エンジン
England igirisu イギリス
English igirisu(jin) no イギリス（人）の
engrave, to kizamu 刻む
enjoy oneself, to tanoshimu 楽しむ
enjoyable tanoshii 楽しい
enlarge, to kakuchôsuru 拡張する
enough jûbun na 十分な
enquire, to tazuneru 尋ねる
enter, to hairu 入る
entire zentai no 全体の
entirety zentai 全体
entrance genkan 玄関, iriguchi 入口
envelope fûtô 封筒
envious urayamashisô na 羨ましそうな
environment kankyô 環境
envy urayamashi sa 羨ましさ
equal dôtô no 同等の
equality byôdô 平等
error machigai 間違い
escalator esukarêtâ エスカレーター
especially toku ni 特に
establish, to setsuritsusuru 設立する, juritsusuru 樹立する
essay shôron 小論, essê エッセー
estimate, to mitsumoru 見積もる
ethnic group minzoku shûdan 民族集団
Europe yôroppa ヨーロッパ
even (also) issô いっそう
even (smooth) nameraka na なめらかな
evening yûgata 夕方
evening meal yûshoku 夕食
event dekigoto 出来事
ever katsute かつて
every (all) subete no 全ての
every (each) ~goto ni ～毎に

every kind of zenshu no 全種の
every time itsumo いつも
everybody, everyone subete no hito 全ての人, bannin 万人
everything subete no mono 全ての物
everywhere dokodemo どこでも
exact, exactly seikaku na 正確な
exactly! sonotôri その通り
exam shiken 試験
examine, to chôsasuru 調査する
example rei 例
example, for tatoeba 例えば
excellent yûshû na 優秀な
except ~o nozoite ～を除いて
exchange (money, opinions) ryôgae 両替, kôkan 交換
exchange, to (money) kankinsuru 換金する
exchange rate kawase sôba 為替相場
excited wakuwakushita わくわくした
exciting wakuwakusaseru わくわくさせる
excuse me! (apology) gomennasai ごめんなさい（謝罪）
excuse me! (attracting attention) sumimasen すみません（注目を引くとき）
excuse me! (getting past) sumimasen すみません（通り抜けるとき）
exist, to sonzaisuru 存在する
exit, to (go out) deru 出る
exit deguchi 出口
expand, to kakudaisuru 拡大する
expect, to yokisuru 予期する
expense hiyô 費用, shuppi 出費
expenses keihi 経費
expensive kôgaku no 高額の, takai 高い
experience keiken 経験
experience, to keikensuru 経験する
expert senmonka 専門家
explain, to setsumeisuru 説明する
export yushutsu 輸出
export, to yushutsusuru 輸出する
express, to noberu 述べる
extension (telephone) denwa no koki 電話の子機, naisen 内線（電話）
extra yobun no 余分の, tokubetsu no 特別の
extremely kyokutan ni 極端に
eye me 目
eyebrow mayuge 眉毛
eyeglasses megane めがね

F

fabric (textile) nuno 布
face kao 顔
face, to chokumensuru 直面する
fact jijitsu 事実
factory kôjô 工場
fail, to shippaisuru 失敗する
failure shippai 失敗
fall (season) aki 秋
fall, to ochiru 落ちる
fall over, to korobu 転ぶ
false (imitation) nise no にせの
false (not true) fuseikaku na 不正確な
family kazoku 家族
famine kiga 飢餓
famous yûmei na 有名な
fan (admirer) fan ファン
fan (for cooling) senpûki 扇風機, uchiwa うちわ
fancy kûsô 空想
far tôku e 遠くへ, tôi 遠い
fare jôsharyôkin 乗車料金
fast (rapid) hayai 速い
fast, to danjikisuru 断食する

fat (grease) shibô 脂肪
fat (plump) futotta 太った
father chichi 父
father-in-law giri no chichi 義理の父
fault kashitsu 過失
fax (machine) fakkusu ファックス
fax (message) fakkusubun ファックス文
fax, to fakkusu o okuru ファックスを送る
fear osore 恐れ
February nigatsu 二月
fee ryôkin 料金, tesûryô 手数料
feed, to tabemono o ataeru 食べ物を与える
feel, to kanjiru 感じる
feeling kanji 感じ
female josei 女性
fence saku 柵
ferry ferî フェリー, watashibune 渡し舟
fertile hiyoku na 肥沃な
festival matsuri 祭り
fetch, to tottekuru 取ってくる
fever hatsunetsu 発熱
few sukunai 少ない
fiancé kon'yakusha 婚約者（女性）
fiancée kon'yakusha 婚約者（男性）
field (empty space) akichi 空き地
fierce araarashii 荒々しい
fifteen jûgo 十五
fifty gojû 五十
fight, to (physically) kenka けんか
fight over, to ~de kenkasuru ～で喧嘩する
figure (number) sûji 数字
fill, to mitasu 満たす
fill out, to (form) kakikomu 書き込む
film (camera) firumu フィルム
film (movie) eiga 映画
final saigo no 最後の
finally saigo ni 最後に
find, to mitsukeru 見つける
fine (healthy) genki na 元気な
fine (punishment) bakkin 罰金
finger yubi 指
finish saigo 最後
finish off, to sumasu 済ます
finished (complete) kanseishita 完成した
finished (none left) owatta 終った
fire honô 炎
fire someone, to kaikosuru 解雇する
fireworks hanabi 花火
firm (definite) dankotoshita 断固とした
firm (mattress) katai 硬い（マットレス）
firm (company) kigyo 企業
first ichiban no 一番の
first mazu まず, hajimeni 初めに
fish sakana 魚
fish, to tsuru 釣る
fish paste kamaboko かまぼこ
fish sauce nanpurâ ナンプラー, gyoshô 魚醤
fit, to gacchisuru 合致する
fitting (suitable) tekisetsu na 適切な
five go 五
fix, to (a time, appointment) kimeru 決める（時間、約束）
fix, to (repair) shûrisuru 修理する
flag hata 旗
flashlight kaichûdentô 懐中電灯
flat (apartment) apâto アパート
flat (smooth) heitan na 平坦な
flight hikô 飛行
flood kôzui 洪水
floor yuka 床
flour komugiko 小麦粉
flower hana 花
flu kaze 風邪, infuruenza インフルエンザ
fluent ryûchô na 流暢な

F

ENGLISH–JAPANESE

flute furûto フルート, fue 笛
fly (insect) hae 蝿
fly, to tobu 飛ぶ
fog kiri 霧
fold, to oru 折る
follow along, to ~ni tsuzuku 〜に続く
follow behind, to ushirokara tsuitekuru 後ろからついてくる
following tsugi no 次の
fond of ~o kononde 〜を好んで
food tabemono 食べ物
foot ashi 足
for ~surutame no 〜するための
for ever eien ni 永遠に
forbid, to kinshisuru 禁止する
forbidden kinjirareta 禁じられた
force chikara 力
force, to shiiru 強いる
forehead odeko おでこ
foreign gaikoku no 外国の
foreigner gaikokujin 外国人
forest mori 森
forget, to wasureru 忘れる
forget about, to ~ni tsuite wasureru 〜について忘れる
forgive, to yurusu 許す
forgiveness kandai sa 寛大さ
forgotten wasurerareta 忘れられた
fork fôku フォーク
form (shape) katachi 形
form (to fill out) yôshi 用紙
fortress yôsai 要塞
fortunately kôunnimo 幸運にも
forty yonjû 四十
forward zenpô ni 前方に
four yon 四
fourteen jûyon 十四
free (independent) dokuritsushita 独立した
free of charge muryô de 無料で
free of restraints museigen ni 無制限に
freedom jiyû 自由
freeze kôritsuku 凍りつく
frequent hinpan na 頻繁な
fresh shinsen na 新鮮な
Friday kinyôbi 金曜日
fried yakareta 焼かれた
friend tomodachi 友達
friendly (outgoing) shakôteki na 社交的な
frightened odoroita 驚いた
from ~kara 〜から
front zenmen 前面
front: in front of ~no mae ni 〜の前に
frown: with a frown kao o shikameta 顔をしかめた
frown, to kao o shikameru 顔をしかめる
frozen kôtta 凍った
fruit kudamono 果物
fry, to yaku 焼く
fulfill, to hatasu 果たす
full ippai no いっぱいの
full (eaten one's fill) onakaga ippai no お腹がいっぱいの
fun: to have fun tanoshimu 楽しむ
function, to (work) kinôsuru 機能する
funds, funding shikin 資金
funeral sôshiki 葬式
fungus shinkinrui 真菌類
funny okashii おかしい
furniture kagu 家具
further (additional) sonoue その上
fussy konomi ni urusai 好みにうるさい
future: in future shôrai 将来

G

gamble kakegoto 賭け事, gyanburu ギャンブル

game shiai 試合
garage (for parking) shako 車庫
garage (for repairs) jidôshashûrikôjô 自動車修理工場
garbage gomi ごみ
garden (yard) niwa 庭
garden (park) kôen 公園
garlic ninniku にんにく
garment irui 衣類
gasoline gasorin ガソリン
gasoline station kyûyujo 給油所
gate mon 門
gather, to atsumeru 集める
gender seibetsu 性別
general (all-purpose) ippanteki na 一般的な
generally ippan ni 一般に
generous kandai na 寛大な
gentle yasashii やさしい
gesture miburi 身振り
get in touch with, to (contact) renrakusuru 連絡する
get, to (receive) uketoru 受け取る
get, to (improve) genki ni naru 元気になる, yokunaru よくなる
get off, to (transport) kôshasuru 降車する
get on, to (transport) jôshasuru 乗車する
get up, to (from bed) okiru 起きる
get well soon hayakunaotte 早く治って
ghost obake お化け
gift okurimono 贈り物
ginger shôga 生姜
girl onna no ko 女の子
girlfriend kanojo 彼女
give, to ataeru 与える
given name na 名（姓に対する名）
glad ureshii うれしい
glass (for drinking) gurasu グラス
glass (material) garasu ガラス
glasses (spectacles) megane めがね
glutinous rice mochigome もち米
go, to iku 行く
go along, to (join) sankasuru 参加する
go around, to (visit) tazuneru 訪ねる
go back modoru 戻る
go for a walk, to sanpo ni iku 散歩に行く
go home, to kitakusuru 帰宅する
go out (fire, candle) kieru 消える（火、ろうそく）
go over, to yokogiru 横切る
go out, to deru 出る
go to bed, to neru 寝る
go up, to (climb) noboru 登る
goal gôru ゴール, mokuhyô 目標
goat yagi 山羊
God kami 神
god gûzô 偶像, kami 神
goddess megami 女神
gold ôgon 黄金
golf gorufu ゴルフ
gone (finished) owatta 終った
good yoi 良い
good luck! kôun o inoru 幸運を祈る
goodbye sayônara さようなら
goodness! aramâ あらまあ
goose gachô ガチョウ
government seifu 政府
gradually jojo ni 徐々に
grand sôdai na 壮大な
grandchild mago 孫
granddaughter magomusume 孫娘
grandfather sofu 祖父
grandmother sobo 祖母
grandparents sofubo 祖父母
grandson magomusuko 孫息子
grapes budô 葡萄
grass kusa 草

G

grateful kanshashita 感謝した
grave haka 墓
grey haiiro no 灰色の
great (grand) sôdai na 壮大な
great (impressive) migoto na 見事な
green midori no 緑の
green beans sayamame さや豆
greens (vegetables) aoyasai 青野菜
greet, to aisatsu o suru 挨拶をする
greetings aisatsu 挨拶
grill, to yaku 焼く
ground jimen 地面
group gurûpu グループ, atsumari 集まり
grow: to be growing (plant) haeru 生える（植物）
grow, to (cultivate) yashinau 養う
grow larger, to ôkikunaru 大きくなる
grow up, to (child) sodatsu 育つ（子供）
guarantee hoshôsho 保証書
guarantee, to hoshôsuru 保証する
guard, to mamoru 守る
guess, to suisokusuru 推測する
guest kyaku 客
guesthouse gêhinkan 迎賓館
guest of honor shuhin 主賓
guide gaido ガイド, annainin 案内人
guidebook ryokôannai 旅行案内
guilty (of a crime) yûzai 有罪
guilty, to feel zaiakukan o kanjiru 罪悪感を感じる

H

hair kami 髪
half hanbun 半分
hall hiroma 広間, genkan 玄関
hand te 手
hand out, to teishutsusuru 提出する
hand over, to watasu 渡す
handicap shôgai 障害
handicraft shukôgei 手工芸
handle totte 取っ手
handsome hansamu ハンサム
hang, to kakeru 掛ける
happen, to okoru 起こる
happened, what nani ga okita 何が起きた
happening dekigoto 出来事
happy shiawase na 幸せな
happy birthday! tanjôbi omedetô 誕生日おめでとう
happy new year! akemashite omedetô 明けましておめでとう
harbor minato 港
hard (difficult) kon'nan na 困難な
hard (solid) katai 固い
hard disk hâdodisuku ハードディスク
hardly hotondo~nai ほとんど〜ない
hardworking kinben na 勤勉な
harmonious chôwa no toreta 調和のとれた
hat bôshi 帽子（つばの広い）
hate, to ken'osuru 嫌悪する
hatred ken'okan 嫌悪感
have, to shoyûsuru 所有する
have already katsute かつて
have been somewhere ~ni ittakoto ga aru 〜に行ったことがある
have done something ~o shitakoto ga aru 〜をしたことがある
have to ~nakute wa ikenai 〜なくてはいけない
he, him kare wa/o 彼は/を
head atama 頭
head for, to (toward) ~e mukau 〜へ向かう
headdress kamikazari 髪飾り
healthy kenkôteki na 健康的な
hear, to kiku 聞く

heart shinzô 心臓
heat, to atatameru 温める
heavy omoi 重い
height takasa 高さ
hello! (on phone) moshimoshi もしもし
hello, hi kon'nichiwa こんにちは
help! tasukete 助けて
help, to tasukeru 助ける, tetsudau 手伝う
her, hers kanojo o/no 彼女を/の
here koko ここ
hidden kakureta 隠れた
hide, to kakusu 隠す
high takai 高い
hill oka 丘
hinder, to samatageru 妨げる
hindrance jama 邪魔, bôgaibutsu 妨害物
hire, to yatou 雇う
his kare no 彼の
history rekishi 歴史
hit (strike) dageki 打撃
hobby shumi 趣味
hold, to (grasp) tsukamu つかむ
hold back, to tamerau ためらう
hole ana 穴
holiday (festival) saijitsu 祭日
holiday (vacation) kyûka 休暇
holy shinsei na 神聖な
home, house ie 家
honest shôjiki na 正直な
honey hachimitsu 蜂蜜
Hong Kong honkon 香港
hope, to nozomu 望む
hopefully kitai o motte 期待をもって
horse uma 馬
hospital byôin 病院
host shujin 主人
hot (spicy) karai 辛い
hot (temperature) atsui 熱い
hot spring onsen 温泉
hotel hoteru ホテル
hour jikan 時間
house ie 家
how? donoyôni どのように
how are you? genkidesuka 元気ですか
however shikashinagara しかしながら
how long? donokurai どのくらい（時間）
how many? donokurai どのくらい（数）
how much? ikura いくら（価格）
how old? ikutsu いくつ（年齢）
huge kyodai na 巨大な
human jinrui 人類
humid shikke no aru 湿気のある
humorous omoshiroi おもしろい
hundred hyaku 百
hundred thousand jûman 十万
hungry kûfuku no 空腹の
hurry up! isoide 急いで
hurt (injured) kizutsuita 傷ついた
hurt, to (cause pain) kizutsuku 傷つく
husband otto 夫
hut (shack) koya 小屋

I

I, me watashi wa/o 私は/を
ice kôri 氷
ice cream aisukurîmu アイスクリーム
idea kangae 考え
identical dôitsu no 同一の
if moshi もし
ignore, to mushisuru 無視する
ignorant muchi no 無知の
illegal fuhô no 不法の
ill byôki no 病気の
illness byôki 病気
imagine, to sôzôsuru 想像する

ENGLISH—JAPANESE

immediately sassoku 早速
impolite shitsurei na 失礼な, burei na 無礼な
import yunyû 輸入
import, to yunyûsuru 輸入する
importance jûyô sa 重要さ
important jûyô na 重要な
impossible fukanô na 不可能な
impression: to make an impression inshôzukeru 印象付ける
impressive migoto na みごとな
in, at (space) ~ni ～に, ~de ～で（空間）
in (time, years) ~no aida ～の間, ~ni ～に（時間、年）
in addition ~ni kuwaete ～に加えて
in order that tame ni ために, yô ni ように
in total zenbu de 全部で
incense okô お香
incident jiken 事件
included, including ~o fukumete ～を含めて
increase zôka 増加
increase, to fuyasu 増やす
indeed! tashika ni 確かに
indigenous koyû no 固有の
Indonesia indoneshia インドネシア
Indonesian indoneshia(jin) no インドネシア（人）の
industrious kinben na 勤勉な
inexpensive yasui 安い, anka na 安価な
influence eikyô 影響
influence, to eikyô o ataeru 影響を与える
inform, to shiraseru 知らせる
information jôhô 情報
information booth annaijo 案内所
inhabitant jûnin 住人, seisokudôbutsu 生息動物
inject, to chûshasuru 注射する
injection chûsha 注射
injured kizutsuita 傷ついた
injury fushô 負傷
ink sumi 墨
insane kyôki no 狂気の
insect konchû 昆虫
inside naibu 内部
inside of ~no naka ni ～の中に
inspect, to tenkensuru 点検する
instead of ~no kawari ni ～の代わりに
instruct, to shijisuru 指示する
instrument dôgu 道具
insult bujoku 侮辱
insult someone, to bujokusuru 侮辱する
insurance hoken 保険
intend, to ~surutsumoridearu ～するつもりである
intended for itosareta 意図された
intention ito 意図
interest kyômi 興味, rishi 利子
interested in ~ni kyômi ga aru ～に興味がある
interesting kyômi bukai 興味深い, omoshiroi 面白い
international kokusaiteki na 国際的な
Internet intânetto インターネット
interpreter tsûyakusha 通訳者
intersection kôsaten 交差点
into ~no naka ni ～の中に
introduce oneself, to jikoshôkaisuru 自己紹介する
introduce someone, to shôkaisuru 紹介する
invent, to hatsumeisuru 発明する
invitation hatsumei 発明
invite, to (ask along) sasou 誘う
invite, to (formally) shôtaisuru 招待する
invoice shikirijô 仕切り状

involve, to tomonau 伴う
involved kan'yoshita 関与した
Ireland airurando アイルランド
Irish airurando(jin) no アイルランド（人）の
iron tetsu no 鉄の
iron, to (clothing) airon o kakeru アイロンをかける（服の）
Islam isuramu イスラム
island shima 島
item (individual thing) hinmoku 品目
ivory zôge 象牙

J

jacket jaketto ジャケット, uwagi 上着
jail keimusho 刑務所
jam jamu ジャム
January ichigatsu 一月
Japan nihon 日本
Japanese nihon(jin) no 日本（人）の
jaw ago あご
jealous shittobukai 嫉妬深い
jealousy shitto 嫉妬
jewellery hôsekirui 宝石類
job shigoto 仕事
join in, to sankasuru 参加する
join, to awaseru 合わせる
join together, to setsuzokusuru 接続する
joke jôku ジョーク, jôdan 冗談
journalist kisha 記者, jânarisuto ジャーナリスト
journey tabi 旅
jug mizusashi 水差し
juice jûsu ジュース, kajû 果汁
July shichigatsu 七月
jump, to tobu 跳ぶ
June rokugatsu 六月
jungle janguru ジャングル, mitsurin 密林
just (fair) kôhei na 公平な
just (only) tatta no たったの
just now tatta ima たった今
just so! sonotôri その通り

K

keep, to tamotsu 保つ
key (computer) kî キー（コンピューター）
key (to room) kagi 鍵（部屋）
keyboard (of computer) kîbôdo キーボード（コンピューター）
kidney jinzôo 腎臓
kidney beans ingenmame インゲン豆
kill, to korosu 殺す
kilogram kiroguramu キログラム
kilometer kiromêtâ キロメーター
kind (of persons) yasashii やさしい（人）
kind (type) shurui 種類
king ôsama 王様
kiss kisu キス, seppun 接吻
kiss, to kisu o suru キスをする
kitchen daidokoro 台所
kiwi fruit kîwifurûtsu キーウィフルーツ
knee hiza 膝
knife kogatana 小刀, naifu ナイフ
knock, to nokkusuru ノックする
know (be acquainted with) chishikiga aru 知識がある
know, to shitteiru 知っている
knowledge chishiki 知識
Korea, North kitachôsen 北朝鮮
Korea, South kankoku 韓国
Korean, North kitachôsen(jin) no 北朝鮮（人）の
Korean, South kankoku(jin) no 韓国（人）の

ENGLISH–JAPANESE

L

lacking kaketeiru 欠けている
ladder hashigo 梯子
ladle shakushi 杓子
lady fujin 婦人
lake mizuumi 湖
lamb hitsujiniku 羊肉, ramu ラム
lamp ranpu ランプ, shômei 照明
land tochi 土地
land, to (plane) chakurikusuru 着陸する（飛行機）
lane komichi 小道
lane (of a highway) shasen 車線（高速道路）
language gengo 言語
Laos raosu ラオス
Laotian raosu(jin) no ラオス（人）の
large hiroi 広い, ôkii 大きい
last saigo no 最後の
last night sakuya 昨夜
last week senshû 先週
last year sakunen 昨年
late osoi 遅い
late at night yoruosoku 夜遅く
later sono go その後, ato de 後で
laugh, to warau 笑う
laugh at, to ~o warau ～を笑う
laws (legislation) hôritsu 法律
lawyer bengoshi 弁護士
lay the table tsukue o naraberu 机を並べる
layer sô 層
lazy taiman na 怠慢な
lead (to guide someone somewhere) annaisuru 案内する
lead, to (as a leader) michibiku 導く
leader shidôsha 指導者
leaf ha 葉
leak, to moreru 漏れる
learn, to narau 習う
least (smallest amount) saishô no 最小の
least: at least sukunakutomo 少なくとも
leather kawa 皮
leave, to shuppatsusuru 出発する
leave behind by accident, to okiwasureru 置き忘れる
leave behind for safekeeping, to hokansuru 保管する
leave behind on purpose, to oiteiku 置いていく
lecture kôgi 講義
lecturer (at university) kôshi（大学の）講師
left (remaining) nokori 残り
left-hand side hidarigawa 左側
leg ashi 脚
legal gôhô no 合法の
legend densetsu 伝説
lemon remon レモン
lemongrass remongurasu レモングラス（香草）
lend, to kasu 貸す
length nagasa 長さ
less (smaller amount) yori sukunaku より少なく
less (minus) ~o hiita ～を引いた
lessen, to sukunakunaru 少なくなる
lesson ressun レッスン, jugyô 授業
let, to kyokasuru 許可する
let someone know, to shiraseru しらせる
let's (suggestion) ~shiyô ～しよう
let's go sâ ikô さあ行こう
letter tegami 手紙
level (even, flat) taira na 平らな
level (height) onajitakasa no 同じ高さの
level (standard) suijun 水準
library toshokan 図書館

license (for driving) menkyoshô 免許証（運転）
license (permit) kyoka 許可
lick, to nameru 舐める
lid futa ふた
lie, to (tell a falsehood) uso o tsuku 嘘をつく
lie down, to nesoberu 寝そべる
life seikatsu 生活
lifetime isshô 一生
lift (elevator) erebêtâ エレベーター
lift, to (something) mochiageru 持ち上げる（物を）
lift, to (ride in car) noseteageru （車に）乗せてあげる
lift, to (raise) takameru 高める
light (bright) akarui 明るい
light (lamp) shômei 照明
light (not heavy) karui 軽い
lighter raitâ ライター
lightning inazuma 稲妻
like (as) ~no yôna ～のような
like (be pleased by) kiniiru 気に入る
likewise onajiyô ni 同じように
lime (citrus) raimu ライム
line (mark) sen 線
line (queue) gyôretsu 行列
line up, to narabu 並ぶ
lips kuchibiru 唇
liquor sake 酒
list hyô 表
listen, to kiku 聴く
listen to ~o kiku ～を聴く
literature bungaku 文学
little (not much) sukunai 少ない
little (small) chiisai 小さい
live, to (be alive) ikiteiru 生きている
live, to (stay in a place) sumu 住む
liver kanzô 肝臓
load tsumini 積み荷
load up, to tsumikomu 積み込む
located, to be ichisuru 位置する
lock jô 錠
lock, to jô o kakeru 錠を掛ける
locked jô no kakatta 錠の掛かった
lodge rojji ロッジ, koya 小屋
lonely sabishii 寂しい
long (length) nagai 長い（距離）
long (time) nagai 長い（時間）
look! mite 見て
look, to ~no yôni omoeu ～のように思える
look after, to sewa o suru 世話をする
look at, to miru 見る
look for, to sagasu 探す
look like, to ~no yôni mieru ～のように見える
look out! ki o tsukete 気をつけて
looks mikake 見かけ
look up, to (find in book) kensakusuru （本を）検索する
loose (not in packet) tabanete inai 束ねていない
loose (wobbly) guratsuita ぐらついた
lose, to (be defeated) makeru 負ける
lose, to (mislay) okiwasureru 置き忘れる
lose money, to kane o nakusu 金をなくす
lost (can't find way) mayotta （道に）迷った
lost (missing) ushinatta 失った
lost property funshitsubutsu 紛失物
lots of takusan no たくさんの
lottery takarakuji 宝くじ
loud onryô no aru 音量のある
love ai 愛
love, to aisuru 愛する, konomu 好む
lovely suteki na 素敵な
low hikui 低い
luck un 運
lucky kôun 幸運
luggage tenimotsu 手荷物

lunch chûshoku 昼食
lunch, to eat chûshoku o toru 昼食をとる
lungs hai 肺
luxurious gôka na 豪華な
lychee raichi ライチ

M

machine kikai 機械
machinery kikairui 機械類
madam (term of address) gofujin ご婦人（女性への敬称）
magazine zasshi 雑誌
mahjong mâjan 麻雀
mail (post) yûbinbutsu 郵便物
mail, to yûsôsuru 郵送する
main (most important) shuyô na 主要な
mainly omo ni 主に
major (important) jûyô na 重要な
make, to tsukuru 作る
make up, to (invent) decchiageru でっち上げる
makeshift maniawase no 間に合わせの
Malaysia marêshia マレーシア
Malaysian marêshia(jin) no マレーシア（人）の
male dansei 男性
man otoko no hito 男の人
manage, to (run) un'eisuru 運営する
manager manêjâ マネージャー
mango mango マンゴ
manufacture, to seizôsuru 製造する
many takusan no たくさんの
map chizu 地図
March sangatsu 三月
market ichiba 市場
married kekkonshita 結婚した
marry: to get married kekkonsuru 結婚する
mask masuku マスク
massage massâji マッサージ
mat matto マット
match macchi マッチ
match (game) shiai 試合
material (ingredient) zairyô 材料
matter (issue) mondai 問題
matter, it doesn't dôdemoii どうでもいい
mattress mattoresu マットレス
May gogatsu 五月
may ~kamoshirenai 〜かもしれない
maybe tabun 多分
meal shokuji 食事
mean (cruel) ijiwarui 意地悪い
mean, to (intend) ~surutsumori 〜するつもり
mean, to (word) imisuru 意味する
meaning imi 意味
meanwhile sono aida ni その間に
measure, to hakaru 計る
measurement sokutê 測定
measure out, to hakari wakeru 計り分ける
meat shokuniku 食肉
meatball nikudango 肉団子
medical igaku no 医学の
medicine iyakuhin 医薬品
meet, to au 会う
meeting kaigô 会合
melon meron メロン
member kaiin 会員
memories kioku 記憶
mend, to naosu 直す
menstruate, to gekkei ga aru 月経がある
mental seishin no 精神の
mention, to noberu 述べる
menu menyû メニュー
merely tan ni 単に
mess: in a mess chirakari 散かり
message dengon 伝言

method hôhô 方法
midday shôgo 正午
midday meal chûshoku 昼食
middle (center) chûô 中央
middle: be in the middle of doing ~no saichû ～の最中
midnight mayonaka 真夜中
might moshikashitara ~kamoshirenai もしかしたら～かもしれない
mild (not severe) odayaka na 穏やかな
mild (not spicy) amakuchi no 甘口の
milk gyûnyû 牛乳
million hyakuman 百万
mind (brain) chiryoku 知力
mind, to (be displeased) ki ni naru 気になる
minibus maikurobasu マイクロバス, kogatabasu 小型バス
minor (not important) taishita koto nai 大したことない
minus ~o hiita ～を引いた
minute fun 分
mirror kagami 鏡
misfortune fukô 不幸
miss, to (bus, flight) noriokureru （バス、飛行機に）乗り遅れる
miss, to (loved one) koishiku omou 恋しく思う
missing (absent) kesseki no 欠席の
missing (lost person) yukuefumei 行方不明
mist kiri 霧
mistake machigai 間違い
mistaken machigae rareta 間違えられた
misunderstanding gokai 誤解
mix, to mazaru 混ざる
mixed kongôshita 混合した
mobile phone keitaidenwa 携帯電話
modern gendai no 現代の
modest (simple) hikaeme na 控えめな
moment: in a moment, just a moment suguni すぐに, shôshô omachi kudasai 少々お待ちください
moment (instant) shunkan 瞬間
Monday getsuyôbi 月曜日
money okane お金
monitor (of computer) monitâ （コンピューターの）モニター
monkey saru 猿
month tsuki 月
monument kinenhi 記念碑
moon tsuki 月
more (comparative) ~yori ôku ～より多く
more of (things) ~yori ôku no ～より多くの
more or less daitai だいたい
morning asa 朝
morning meal chôshoku 朝食
mosque mosuku モスク
mosquito ka 蚊
most (superlative) mottomo 最も
most (the most of) hotondo ほとんど
mostly daibubun wa 大部分は
moth ga 蛾
mother haha 母
mother-in-law girinohaha 義理の母
motor, engine motâ モーター, enjin エンジン
motor vehicle dôryokusha 動力車
motorcycle ôtobai オートバイ, tansha 単車
mountain yama 山
mouse (animal) nezumi ねずみ
mouse (computer) mausu マウス（コンピューター）
moustache kuchihige 口ひげ
mouth kuchi 口
move, to ugoku 動く
move from one place to, to ~kara ~ni idôsuru ～から～に移動する

M

ENGLISH—JAPANESE

movement (motion) ugoki 動き
movie eiga 映画
movie house eigakan 映画館
much takusan no たくさんの
murder, to korosu 殺す
muscle kinniku 筋肉
mushroom kinoko きのこ
music ongaku 音楽
Muslim isuramukyô(to) no イスラム教（徒）の
must ~nakutewaikenai 〜なくてはいけない
mutton maton マトン
my, mine watashi no 私の
Myanmar myanmâ ミャンマー
myth shinwa 神話

N

nail (finger, toe) tsume 爪（手、足）
nail (spike) kugi 釘
naked hadaka no 裸の
name namae 名前
named yobareteiru 呼ばれている
narrow semai 狭い
nation (country) kuni 国
national kuni no 国の
nationality kokuseki 国籍
natural shizen no 自然の
nature shizen 自然
naughty itazura na いたずらな, wanpaku na 腕白な
nearby sugusoba no すぐそばの
nearly hotondo ほとんど
neat (orderly) kichintoshita きちんとした
necessary hitsuyô na 必要な
neck kubi 首
necklace kubikazari 首飾り
necktie nekutai ネクタイ
need hitsuyô 必要
need, to hitsuyô de aru 必要である
needle hari 針
neighbor rinjin 隣人
neither ~de nai 〜でない
neither … nor ~mo~mo~nai 〜も〜も〜ない
nephew oi 甥
nest su 巣
net ami 網
network hôsômô 放送網, kairomô 回路網
never kesshite~nai 決して〜ない
never mind! ki ni shinaide 気にしないで
nevertheless sorenimo kakawarazu それにもかかわらず
new atarashii 新しい
New Zealand nyûjîrando ニュージーランド
news nyûsu ニュース
newspaper shinbun 新聞
next (in line, sequence) tsugi no 次の
next to tonari ni 隣に
next week raishû 来週
next year rainen 来年
nice suteki na 素敵な
niece mei 姪
night yoru 夜
nightclothes, nightdress nemaki 寝巻き
nightly yogoto no 夜毎の
nine kyû 九
nineteen jûkyû 十九
ninety kyûjû 九十
no, not (with nouns) ~dewa nai 〜ではない（名詞につく）
no, not (with verbs and adjectives) ~nai 〜ない, ~dewanai 〜ではない（動詞と形容詞につく）
nobody daremo~nai 誰も〜ない
noise oto 音
noisy urusai うるさい

nonsense muimi na kotoba 無意味な言葉, nansensu ナンセンス
noodles menrui 麺類
noon shôgo 正午
nor ~demo nai ～でもない
normal futsû no 普通の
normally futsû wa 普通は
north kita 北
north-east hokutô 北東
north-west hokusei 北西
nose hana 鼻
nostril bikô 鼻腔
not ~dewa nai ～ではない
not only … but also ~dake de naku~mo mata ～だけでなく～もまた
not yet madadesu まだです
note (currency) shihei 紙幣
note (written) memo メモ
note down, to kaki tomeru 書き留める
notebook nôto ノート
nothing nanimo~nai 何も～ない
notice chûmoku 注目, chûi 注意
notice, to kizuku 気づく
novel shôsetsu 小説
November jûichigatsu 十一月
now ima 今
nowadays kon'nichi de wa 今日では
nowhere dokonimo~nai どこにも～ない
nude hadaka 裸
numb mahishita 麻痺した
number kazu 数
nylon nairon ナイロン

O

o'clock ~ji ～時
obedient jûjun na 従順な
obey, to shitagau 従う
object (thing) buttai 物体
object, to (protest) hantaisuru 反対する
occasionally tamani たまに
occupation shokugyô 職業
occur, to okoru 起こる
ocean umi 海
October jûgatsu 十月
odor (bad smell) akushû 悪臭
of (from) ~no ～の, ~kara ～から
of course mochiron もちろん
off (gone bad) warukunatte 悪くなって
off (turned off) keshita 消した, tomatta 止まった
off: to turn something off keshita 消した
offend, to kanjô o gaisuru 感情を害する
offer, to (suggest) teikyôsuru 提供する
offering teikyô 提供
office jimusho 事務所, ofisu オフィス
official (formal) kôshiki no 公式の
officials (government) yakunin 役人（政府）
often shibashiba しばしば, yoku よく
oil abura 油
okay ii いい, ôkê オーケー
old (of persons) toshitotta 年取った（人）
old (of things) furui 古い（物）
old times, in mukashi wa 昔は
older brother chôkei 長兄
older sister chôshi 長姉
on (of dates) ~ni ～に, ~no toki ni ～の時に
on (turned on) haitta 入った
on (at) ~no ue ni ～の上に, ~ni ～に
on: to turn something on tsuketa 点けた
on board ~ni notte ～に乗って

O

ENGLISH—JAPANESE

on fire hi ga tsuita 火がついた
on foot toho de 徒歩で
on the way tochû de 途中で
on the whole zentai kara mite 全体からみて
on time jikan dôri ni 時間通りに
once ichido 一度
one ichi 一
one-way ticket katamichi kippu 片道切符
onion tamanegi 玉葱
only tatta~dake たった～だけ
open hiraiteiru 開いている
open, to akeru 開ける
opinion iken 意見
opponent taikôsha 対抗者
opportunity kikai 機会
oppose, to hantaisuru 反対する
opposed, in opposition hantai no 反対の
opposite (contrary) ~ni hanshite ～に反して
opposite (facing) hantai gawa no 反対側の
optional zuii no 随意の
or ~ka~ ～か～
orange (color) orenjiiro オレンジ色
orange (citrus) orenji オレンジ
order (command) meirei 命令
order (placed for food, goods) chûmon 注文（食べ物や物）
order (sequence) junban 順番
order, to (command) meireisuru 命令する
order something, to chûmonsuru 注文する
orderly (organized) seitonsareta 整とんされた
organize, to chôseisuru 調整する
origin kigen 起源
original genkei no 原型の
originate, to (come from) ~kara okoru ～から起こる
ornament sôshokuhin 装飾品
other hoka no 他の
ought to ~subeki de aru ～すべきである
our wareware no 我々の
out ~no soto e ～の外へ
outside sotogawa 外側
outside of ~no soto ni ～の外に
oval (shape) daenkei 楕円形
oven tenpi 天火, ôbun オーブン
over (finished) owatta 終った
over: to turn over uragaesu 裏返す
over there achira gawa あちら側, asoko あそこ
overcast (cloudy) kumotta 曇った
overcome, to uchikatsu 打ち勝つ
overseas kaigai no 海外の
overturned hikkurikaetta ひっくり返った
owe, to kari ga aru 借りがある
own, to shojisuru 所持する
own (personal) jibun no 自分の
own: on one's own hitori de 独りで
oyster kaki 牡蠣

P

pack, package tsutsumi 包み
page pêji 頁
paid yûkyû no 有給の
pain itami 痛み
painful itai 痛い
paint penki ペンキ, ganryô 顔料
paint, to (a painting) e o kaku 描く（絵）
paint, to (house, furniture) penki o nuru ペンキを塗る（家、家具）
painting kaiga 絵画
pair of, a ittsui no 一対の

pajamas nemaki 寝巻き, pajama パジャマ
palace kyûden 宮殿
pan nabe 鍋
panorama zenkei 全景, panorama パノラマ
panties pantî パンティー
pants zubon ズボン
papaya papaiya パパイヤ
paper kami 紙
parcel kozutsumi 小包
pardon me? what did you say shitsurei, nante osshai mashita ka 失礼、何ておっしゃいましたか
parents ryôshin 両親
park kôen 公園
park, to (car) chûsha suru 駐車する
part (not whole) ichibu 一部
part (of machine) buhin 部品
participate, to sankasuru 参加する
particularly toku ni 特に
partly bubunteki ni 部分的に
partner (in business) kyôdô keieisha 共同経営者
partner (spouse) tsureai つれあい
party (event) pâtî パーティー（催し）
party (political) tô 党（政治的な）
pass, to (exam) gôkakusuru 合格する（試験）
pass, to (go past) tôrikosu 通り越す
passenger jôkyaku 乗客
passionfruit tokeisô no kajitsu トケイソウの果実, passhonfurûtsu パッションフルーツ
passport ryoken 旅券, pasupôto パスポート
past: go past tôrikosu 通り越す
past (former) mukashi no 昔の
pastime goraku 娯楽
patient (calm) nintai no aru 忍耐のある
patient (doctor's) kanja 患者
pattern (design) moyô 模様, gara 柄
patterned moyô no aru 模様のある
pay, to harau 払う
pay attention chûi o harau 注意を払う
payment shiharai 支払い
peace heiwa 平和
peaceful heiwa na 平和な
peak (summit) sanchô 山頂, chôten 頂点
peanut pînattsu ピーナッツ
pearl shinju 真珠
peas endômame エンドウ豆
peel, to muku 剥く
pen pen ペン
pencil enpitsu 鉛筆
penis penisu ペニス
people hitobito 人々
pepper (black) kurokoshô 黒胡椒
pepper (chilli) tôgarashi 唐辛子
percent, percentage hyakubunritsu 百分率, pâsento パーセント
performance kôen 公演, dekibae 出来映え
perfume kôsui 香水
perhaps (maybe) tabun 多分
perhaps (probably) osoraku おそらく
period (end of a sentence) kutôten 句読点
period (menstrual) seiri 生理
period (of time) kikan 期間
permanent eikyû no 永久の
permit (license) menkyo 免許
permit, to (allow) kyokasuru 許可する
person hito 人
personality kosei 個性, seikaku 性格
perspire, to ase o kaku 汗をかく
pet animal aiganddubutsu 愛玩動物, petto ペット
petrol gasorin ガソリン

petrol station kyûyujo 給油所, gasorin sutando ガソリンスタンド
pharmacy yakkyoku 薬局
Philippines firipin フィリピン
photocopy kopî コピー
photocopy, to kopîsuru コピーする
photograph shashin 写真
photograph, to shashin o toru 写真を撮る
pick, to (choose) erabu 選ぶ
pick up, to (someone) kuruma ni noseru 車に乗せる（人を）
pick up, to (something) mochiageru 持ち上げる（物を）
pickpocket suri すり
pickpocket, to suru する
picture e 絵
piece (item) ikko 一個
piece (portion, section) hitokire ひと切れ
pierce, to tsukitôsu 突き通す
pig buta 豚
pillow makura 枕
pills jôzai 錠剤
pineapple painappuru パイナップル
pink pinku no ピンクの
pitcher mizusashi 水差し
pity: what a pity zannen da 残念だ
place basho 場所
place, to oku 置く
plain (level ground) taira na 平らな
plain (not fancy) heibon na 平凡な
plan keikaku 計画
plan, to keikakusuru 計画する
plane hikôki 飛行機
plant shokubutsu 植物
plant, to ueru 植える
plastic purasuchikku プラスチック
plate sara 皿
play, to ~suru ～する
play around, to asobimawaru 遊びまわる
plead, to kongansuru 懇願する
pleasant kanjinoii 感じのいい
please (go ahead) dôzo どうぞ（勧めるとき）
please (request for help) onegai shimasu お願いします（助けを依頼する時）
please (request for something) onegai shimasu お願いします（何かを依頼する時）
pleased manzokushita 満足した
plug (bath) sen 栓（風呂）
plug (electric) sashikomi 差込, puragu プラグ（電気）
plum puramu プラム
plus tsukekuwawatta 付け加わった, purasu プラス
pocket poketto ポケット
point (in time) jiten 時点（時間）
point(dot) ten 点
point out shitekisuru 指摘する
poison doku 毒
poisonous dokusei no 毒性の
police keisatsu 警察
police officer keisatsukan 警察官
polish, to migaku 磨く
politics seiji 政治
polite reigitadashii 礼儀正しい
poor mazushii 貧しい
popular ninki no aru 人気のある
population jinkô 人口
pork butaniku 豚肉
port minato 港
portion (serve) wakemae 分け前
possess, to shoyûsuru 所有する
possessions shoyûbutsu 所有物
possible kanô na 可能な
possibly osoraku~darô おそらく～だろう
post (column) hashira 柱
post (mail) yûbin 郵便
postcard hagaki 葉書

postpone, to enkisuru 延期する
postponed enkishita 延期した
post office yûbinkyoku 郵便局
pot hachi 鉢
potato jagaimo ジャガイモ
poultry shokuyô no tori 食用の鳥
pour, to sosogu 注ぐ
power chikara 力
powerful chikarazuyoi 力強い
practice shûkan 習慣, renshû 練習
practise, to renshûsuru 練習する
praise shôsan 賞賛
praise, to shôsansuru 賞賛する
prawn ebi 海老
pray, to inoru 祈る
prayer kigan(suruhito) 祈願（する人）
prefer, to konomu 好む
pregnant ninshinshita 妊娠した
prepare, to (**make ready**) junbisuru 準備する
prepared (ready) yôi ga dekiteiru 用意ができている
prescription shohôsen 処方箋
present (gift) okurimono 贈り物, purezento プレゼント
present, to be (here) koko ni iru ここにいる
present, to okurimono o suru 贈り物をする
present: at the present moment genzai 現在
presently (nowadays) genzai 現在
preserved hozonsareta 保存された
president daitôryô 大統領, kaichô 会長, shachô 社長
press (journalism) shinbun 新聞
press, to osu 押す
pressure atsuryoku 圧力
pretend, to ~o yosoou ～を装う
pretty (of places, things) utsukushii 美しい, kogirei na こぎれいな（場所、物）
pretty (of women) kawairashii かわいらしい（女性）
pretty (very) totemo とても
prevent, to samatageru 妨げる
price nedan 値段
pride hokori 誇り, jisonshin 自尊心
priest shisai 司祭
prime minister shushô 首相
print, to insatsusuru 印刷する
prison keimusho 刑務所
private kojinteki na 個人的な
probably osoraku おそらく
problem mondai 問題
produce, to seisansuru 生産する
profession shokugyô 職業
profit rieki 利益
program (schedule) yotei 予定
promise, to yakusokusuru 約束する
pronounce, to hatsuonsuru 発音する
proof shôko 証拠
property shisan 資産
protest, to hantaisuru 反対する
proud hokori ni omou 誇りに思う
prove, to shômeisuru 証明する
public kôkyô no 公共の
publish, to shuppansuru 出版する
pull, to hiku 引く
pump ponpu ポンプ, asshukuki 圧縮機
punctual jikandôri no 時間どおりの
pupil seito 生徒
pure junsui na 純粋な
purple murasaki 紫
purpose mokuteki 目的
purse (for money) saifu 財布（お金）
push, to osu 押す
put, to (place) oku 置く
put off (delay) enkisuru 延期する
put on (clothes) kiru 着る（服を）
put together, to kumiawaseru 組み合わせる
puzzled konwakushita 困惑した

Q

ENGLISH–JAPANESE

Q

qualification shikaku 資格
quarter yonbun no ichi 四分の一
queen joô 女王
question shitsumon 質問
queue (line) retsu 列
queue, to (line up) retsu o tsukuru 列をつくる
quick kibin na 機敏な, hayai 速い
quickly binsoku ni 敏速に
quiet shizuka na 静かな
quite (fairly) kanari かなり
quite (very) zuibun ずいぶん

R

radio rajio ラジオ
rail: by rail ressha de 列車で
railroad, railway senro 線路, tetsudo 鉄道
rain ame 雨
rain, to ame ga furu 雨が降る
raise, to (children) sodateru 育てる（子供）
raise, to (lift) ageru 揚げる
rank (station in life) kaikyû 階級
ranking jôretsu 序列
rapid hayai 速い
rare (scarce) mezurashii 珍しい
rare (half-cooked) namayake no 生焼けの
rarely, seldom mare ni まれに
rat nezumi ねずみ
rate (tariff) ryôkin 料金
rate of exchange (for foreign currency) kawase rêto 為替レート
rather (fairly) kanari no かなりの
rather than ~yori mushiro 〜よりむしろ
raw (uncooked) nama no 生の
reach, to (get to) tôchakusuru 到着する
react, to hannôsuru 反応する
read, to yomu 読む
ready yôidekita 用意できた
ready: to get/make ready junbisuru 準備する
realize, to satoru 悟る
really (in fact) jissai ni 実際に
really (truly, honestly) hontô ni 本当に
really? hontô 本当
rear (tail) ushiro 後ろ
reason riyû 理由
reasonable (price) tegoro na 手ごろな（値段）
reasonable (sensible) bunbetsu no aru 分別のある
receipt ryôshûsho 領収書
receive, to uketoru 受け取る
recipe reshipi レシピ
reckon, to kazoeru 数える
recognize, to mitomeru 認める
recommend, to susumeru 勧める
recovered (cured) kaifukushita 回復した
rectangle chôhôkei 長方形
red aka 赤
reduce, to herasu 減らす
reduction genshô 減少
reflect, to hankyôsuru 反響する
refreshment (drink) nomimono 飲み物
refrigerator reizôko 冷蔵庫
refusal kyozetsu 拒絶
refuse, to kotowaru 断る
regarding ~ni kanshite 〜に関して
region chiiki 地域
register, to tôrokusuru 登録する
registered post kakitome 書留
regret, to kôkaisuru 後悔する
regrettably oshikumo 惜しくも
regular (normal) tsûjô no 通常の

relatives shinseki 親戚
relax, to kutsurogu くつろぐ
release, to hanasu 放す
religion shûkyô 宗教
remainder (leftover) nokorimono 残り物
remains (historical) iseki 遺跡（歴史的）
remember, to oboeteiru 覚えている
remind, to omoidasaseru 思い出させる
rent, to kasu 貸す
rent out, to chingashisuru 賃貸しする
repair, to shûrisuru 修理する
repeat, to kurikaesu 繰り返す
replace, to irekawaru 入れ替わる
reply (response) henji 返事
reply, to (in speech) hentôsuru 返答する
reply, to (in writing) henji o kaku 返事を書く
report hôkoku 報告
report, to hôkokusuru 報告する
reporter repôtâ レポーター
request, to (formally) iraisuru 依頼する（公式に）
request, to (informally) tanomu 頼む（非公式に）
rescue, to kyûjosuru 救助する
research kenkyû 研究
research, to kenkyûsuru 研究する
resemble ruijisuru 類似する
reservation yoyaku 予約
reserve (for animals) hogoku 保護区（動物）
reserve, to (ask for in advance) yoyakusuru 予約する
resident jûnin 住人
resolve, to (a problem) kaiketsusuru 解決する（問題）
respect sonkei 尊敬
respect, to sonkeisuru 尊敬する
respond, to hentôsuru 返答する
response (reaction) hentô 返答, hannô 反応
responsibility sekinin 責任
responsible, to be sekinin o motsu 責任を持つ
rest (remainder) nokori 残り
rest, to (relax) yasumu 休む
restaurant resutoran レストラン
restrain, to osaeru 抑える
restroom tearai 手洗い
result: as a result, resulting from ~no kekkatoshite ～の結果として
result kekka 結果
result (effect) eikyô 影響
return, to (give back) kaesu 返す
return, to (go back) modoru 戻る
retired intaishita 引退した
return ticket ôfukukippu 往復キップ
return to one's home town, to kikyôsuru 帰郷する
reveal, to (make known) akiraka ni suru 明らかにする
reveal, to (make visible) arawasu 現す
reverse, to (go backwards) gyakkôsuru 逆行する
reversed sakasama no 逆さまの
ribbon ribon リボン
rice (cooked) gohan ご飯（炊いた）
rice (plant) ine 稲
rice (uncooked) kome 米
rice fields tanbo 田んぼ
rich kanemochi no 金持ちの
rid: get rid of torinozoku 取り除く
ride, to (in car, on an animal) noru （車、動物に）乗る
ride, to (transport) jôshasuru （乗り物に）乗車する
right (correct) tadashii 正しい
right-hand side migigawa 右側

R

ENGLISH–JAPANESE

right now suguni すぐに
rights kenri 権利
ring (jewellery) yubiwa 指輪
ring, to (bell) narasu （ベルを）鳴らす
ring, to (on the telephone) denwasuru 電話する
ripe jukushita 熟した
rise (ascendance) jôshô 上昇
rise (increase) zôka 増加
rival kyôsôaite 競争相手
river kawa 川
road michi 道
roast, to (grill) aburu あぶる
roasted (grilled) aburareta あぶられた
rock ishi 石
role yakuwari 役割
roof yane 屋根
room (in hotel/house) heya 部屋（ホテル/家）
room (space) kûkan 空間
root (of plant) ne 根（植物）
rope rôpu ロープ, nawa 縄
rotten kusatta 腐った
rough arappoi 荒っぽい
roughly (approximately) ôyoso おおよそ
round (around) ôyoso no おおよその
round (shape) marui 丸い
rubber gomu ゴム
rude shitsurei na 失礼な
ruined hakaisareta 破壊された
rule kisoku 規則
run, to hashiru 走る
run away, to nigeru 逃げる

S

sacred shinês na 神聖な
sacrifice gisei 犠牲
sacrifice, to gisei ni suru 犠牲にする
sad kanashii 悲しい
safe anzen na 安全な
sail, to funatabi o suru 船旅をする
salary kyûryô 給料
sale, for urimono 売りもの
sale (reduced prices) yasuuri 安売り, bâgen バーゲン
sales assistant ten'in 店員
salt shio 塩
salty shiokarai 塩辛い
same onaji 同じ
sample mihon 見本
sand suna 砂
sandals sandaru サンダル
satisfied manzokushita 満足した
satisfy, to manzokusaseru 満足させる
Saturday doyôbi 土曜日
sauce sôsu ソース
sauce (chilli) chirisôsu チリソース
save, to tamotsu 保つ
say, to iu 言う
say hello, to konnichiwa to iu こんにちはと言う, yoroshiku よろしく
say goodbye, to sayônara to iu さようならと言う
say sorry, to ayamaru 謝る
say thank you, to arigatô to iu ありがとうと言う
scales hakari はかり
scarce toboshii 乏しい
scared obieta おびえた
scenery keshiki 景色
schedule kêkaku 計画
school gakkô 学校
schoolchild gakudô 学童
science kagaku 科学
scissors hasami はさみ
Scotland sukottorando スコットランド
Scottish, Scots sukottorando(jin) no スコットランド（人）の

screen (of computer) gamen 画面, sukurîn スクリーン（コンピューター）
scrub, to araiotosu 洗い落とす
sculpt, to chôkokusuru 彫刻する
sculpture chôkoku 彫刻
sea umi 海
seafood kaisanbutsu 海産物
search for, to ~o sagasu ～を探す
season kisetsu 季節
seat isu 椅子
second byô 秒, daini no 第二の
secret himitsu 秘密
secret: to keep a secret himitsu o mamoru 秘密を守る
secretary hisho 秘書
secure anzen na 安全な
see, to miru 見る
seed tane 種
seek, to motomeru 求める
seem, to ~to omowareru ～と思われる
see you later! soredewa mata それではまた
seldom hotondo~nai ほとんど～ない
select, to erabu 選ぶ
self jishin 自身
sell, to uru 売る
send, to okuru 送る
sensible shiryo no aru 思慮のある
sentence bun 文, sentensu センテンス
separate wakareta 分かれた
separate, to wakeru 分ける
September kugatsu 九月
sequence (order) junjo 順序
serious (not funny) majime na まじめな
serious (severe) hidoi ひどい
servant meshitsukai 召使
serve, to tsukaeru 仕える
service hôshi 奉仕
sesame oil goma abura ゴマ油
sesame seeds goma ゴマ
set shotei no 所定の
set up, to setsuritsusuru 設立する, juritsusuru 樹立する
seven nana, shichi 七
seventeen jûnana, jûshichi 十七
seventy nanajû 七十
several ikutsuka no いくつかの
severe kibishii きびしい
sew, to nuu 縫う
sex (gender) seibetsu 性別
sex, sexual activity seikô 性交, sekkusu セックス
shack koya 小屋
shade kage 陰
shadow kage 影
shadow play kagee 影絵
shake, to furu 振る
shall ~deshô ～でしょう
shallow asai 浅い
shame (disgrace) chijoku 恥辱
shame: what a shame! zannen 残念
shampoo shanpû シャンプー
shape katachi 形
shape, to (form) katachizukuru 形作る
shark same 鮫
sharp surudoi 鋭い
shatter, to konagona ni suru 粉々にする
shave, to soru 剃る
she, her kanojo wa/o 彼女は/を
sheet (for bed) shîtsu シーツ
sheet (of paper) ichimai no kami 一枚の紙
sheep hitsuji 羊
Shinto shintô 神道
shiny hikaru 光る
ship fune 船

shirt shatsu シャツ
shit daiben 大便, kuso くそ
shiver, to miburuisuru 身震いする
shoes kutsu 靴
shoot, to utsu 撃つ
shop, to (go shopping) kaimono o suru 買い物をする
shop mise 店
shopkeeper ten'in 店員
short (concise) mijikai 短い
short (not tall) hikui 低い
short time (a moment) tanjikan 短時間
shorts (short trousers) shôtsu ショーツ, tanpan 短パン
shorts (underpants) pantsu パンツ（下着）
shoulder kata 肩
shout, to sakebu 叫ぶ
show (broadcast) bangumi 番組
show (live performance) shô ショー, moyôshi 催し
show, to miseru 見せる
shower (for washing) shawâ シャワー
shower (of rain) kosame 小雨
shower: to take a shower shawâ o abiru シャワーを浴びる
shrimp ebi 海老
shut shimatta 閉まった
shut, to tojiru 閉じる
sibling kyôdai きょうだい
sick byôki no 病気の
sick, to be (vomit) hakike ga suru 吐き気がする
side yoko 横
sightseeing kankô 観光
sign (symbol) hyôshiki 標識
sign, to shomei suru 署名する
signature shomei 署名, sain サイン
signboard kanban 看板
silent mugon no 無言の
silk kinu 絹
silver gin 銀
similar ruijishita 類似した
simple (uncomplicated, modest) jimi na 地味な
simple (easy) kantan na 簡単な
since irai 以来
sing, to utau 歌う
Singapore shingapôru シンガポール
single (not married) dokushin no 独身の
single (only one) yuiitsu no 唯一の
sir (term of address) kika 貴下（男性への敬称）
sister shimai 姉妹
sister-in-law (older brother's wife or husband's older sister) gishi 義姉
sister-in-law (younger brother's wife or husband's younger sister) gimai 義妹
sit, to suwaru 座る
sit down, to suwaru 座る
situated, to be ~no jôtai ni aru ～の状態にある
situation (how things are) jôkyô 状況
six roku 六
sixteen jûroku 十六
sixty rokujû 六十
size saizu サイズ
skewer yakigushi 焼き串
skillful jukurenshita 熟練した
skin hada 肌
skirt sukâto スカート
sky sora 空
sleep, to neru 寝る
sleepy nemui 眠い
slender hosoi 細い, sumâto na スマートな
slight wazuka na わずかな
slightly wazuka ni わずかに

slim surimu na スリムな, hosoi 細い
slip (petticoat, underskirt) surippu スリップ, pechikôto ペチコート
slippers surippa スリッパ, uwabaki 上履き
slope saka 坂
slow osoi 遅い
slowly yukkuri ゆっくり
small chîsai 小さい
small change kozeni 小銭
smart kashikoi 賢い
smell (bad odor) akushû 悪臭
smell, to niou 臭う
smile, to warau 笑う
smoke kemuri 煙
smoke, to (tobacco) tabako o suu タバコをすう
smooth (of surfaces) subesubeshita すべすべした
smooth (to go smoothly) enkatsu ni susumu 円滑にすすむ
smuggle, to mitsuyunyûsuru 密輸入する
snake hebi 蛇
snapped (of bones, etc.) oreta 折れた（骨など）
sneeze kushami くしゃみ
sneeze, to kushami o suru くしゃみをする
snow yuki 雪
snow, to yuki ga furu 雪が降る
snowpeas sunôendô スノーエンドウ
so (therefore) sorede それで, soreyue それゆえ
so (very) totemo とても
so that dakara だから, ~suru tame ni 〜するために
soak, to hitaru 浸る
soap sekken 石鹸
soccer sakkâ サッカー
socket (electric) soketto ソケット, ukeguchi 受け口（電気の）
socks kutsushita 靴下
sofa sofâ ソファー, nagaisu 長いす
soft yawarakai やわらかい
soft drink seiryôinryôsui 清涼飲料
soil tsuchi 土
sold urareta 売られた
sold out urikire 売り切れ
soldier heitai 兵隊
sole (only) tatta hitotsu no たったひとつの
solid kotai no 固体の
solve, to (a problem) kaiketsusuru 解決する（問題を）
some ikutsuka no いくつかの
somebody, someone dareka 誰か
something nanika 何か
sometimes tokidoki 時々
somewhere dokoka どこか
son musuko 息子
son-in-law giri no musuko 義理の息子
song uta 歌
soon sugu ni すぐに
sore, painful itai 痛い
sorrow kanashimi 悲しみ
sorry gomennasai ごめんなさい
sorry, to (feel regretful) kôkaisuru 後悔する
sort (type) shurui 種類
sort out, to taishosuru 対処する
sound oto 音
soup (clear) sûpu スープ
soup (spicy stew) shichû シチュー, nikomi 煮込み
sour suppai すっぱい
source minamoto 源
south minami 南
south-east nantô 南東
south-west nansei 南西
souvenir miyagemono みやげ物
soy sauce (salty) shôyu しょう油

S

ENGLISH—JAPANESE

S

ENGLISH–JAPANESE

space kûkan 空間
spacious hirobiroshita 広々した
speak, to hanasu 話す
special tokubetsu na 特別な
spectacles sôkan 壮観
spectacles (glasses) megane めがね
speech supîchi スピーチ
speech: to make a speech supîchi o suru スピーチをする
speed supîdo スピード
spell, to tsuzuru 綴る
spend, to tsuiyasu 費やす
spices kôshinryô 香辛料
spicy karai 辛い
spinach hôrensô ほうれん草
spine sebone 背骨
spiral rasenjô no らせん状の
spirits (hard liquor) jôryûshu 蒸留酒
spoiled (does not work) kowareta 壊れた
spoiled (of food) kusatta 腐った（食べ物）
spoon supûn スプーン
sponge suponji スポンジ
sports supôtsu no スポーツの, undôyô no 運動用の
spotted (pattern) mizutamamoyô no 水玉もようの（柄）
spray supurê スプレー
spring (metal part) supuringu スプリング, danryoku 弾力
spring (of water) wakimizu 湧き水
spring (season) haru 春
split up, to bunkatsusuru 分割する
spouse haigûsha 配偶者
square (shape) shikakui 四角い
square (town square) hiroba 広場
squid ika イカ
staff sutaffu スタッフ, ichiin 一員
stain shimi しみ
stairs kaidan 階段
stall (of vendor) baiten 売店
stall, to (car) shissoku saseru 失速させる（車）
stamp (ink) kokuin 刻印, sutanpu スタンプ
stamp (postage) kitte （郵便）切手
stand, to tatsu 立つ
stand up, to tachiagaru 立ち上がる
star hoshi 星
start (beginning) hajimari 始まり
start, to hajimeru 始める
state, to noberu 述べる
stationery bunbôgu 文房具
statue zô 像
stay, to (remain) nokoru 残る
stay overnight, to ippakusuru 一泊する
steal, to nusumu 盗む
steam jôki 蒸気
steamed musareta 蒸された
steel hagane はがね
steer, to kaji o toru かじをとる
step ashidori 足取り, ippo 一歩
steps, stairs kaidan 階段
stick (pole) bô 棒
stick out, to depparu 出っ張る
stick to, to ~ni haru ～に貼る
sticky nebanebashita ねばねばした
sticky rice mochigome もち米
stiff katai 堅い
still (even now) mada まだ
still (quiet) shizuka na 静かな
stink, to akushû o hanatsu 悪臭を放つ
stomach hara 腹
stone ishi 石
stool koshikake 腰掛, benki 便器
stop (bus, train) teiryûjo 停留所, eki 駅（バス、電車の）
stop, to (cease) yameru やめる
stop, to (halt) tomeru 止める
stop by, to (pay a visit) tazuneru 訪ねる

stop it yamete やめて
store (saving) takuwae 蓄え
store, shop mise 店
storey (of a building) kai 階（建物）
storm arashi 嵐
story (tale) hanashi 話
stout zungurishita ずんぐりした
stove (cooker) konro コンロ, kamado かまど
straight (not crooked) massugu na 真っ直ぐな
straight ahead massugu mae ni 真っ直ぐ前に
strait kaikyô 海峡
strange hen na 変な
stranger shiranai hito 知らない人
street michi 道, tôri 通り
strength chikara 力
strict kibishii 厳しい
strike, to (hit) utsu 打つ
strike: to go on strike sutoraiki o suru ストライキをする
string himo 紐
striped shima no aru 縞のある
strong tsuyoi 強い
stubborn (determined) ganko na 頑固な
stuck (won't move) koteisareta 固定された
student gakusei 学生
study, to gakushûsuru 学習する
stupid oroka na 愚かな
style katachi 形
succeed, to seikôsuru 成功する
success seikô 成功
such ~no yôna ～のような
such as ~no yôna ～のような, tatoeba 例えば
suck, to suu 吸う
suddenly kyûni 急に
suffer, to kurushimu 苦しむ
suffering kurushimi 苦しみ
sugar satô 砂糖
sugarcane satôkibi サトウキビ
suggest, to teian suru 提案する
suggestion teian 提案
suit (business) sûtsu スーツ
suitable fusawashii ふさわしい, oniai no お似合いの
suitcase sûtsukêsu スーツケース
summer natsu 夏
summit (peak) sanchô 山頂
summon, to yobidasu 呼び出す
sun taiyô 太陽
Sunday nichiyôbi 日曜日
sunlight hizashi 日差し
sunny hiatari ga ii 日当たりがいい
sunrise hinode 日の出
sunset hinoiri 日の入
supermarket sûpâmâketto スーパーマーケット
suppose, to ~dato omou ～だと思う
sure kakushinshita 確信した
surf uchiyoseru nami 打ち寄せる波, sâfin サーフィン
surface hyômen 表面
surface mail futsûyûbin 普通郵便
surname myôji 苗字
surprised odoroita 驚いた
surprising odorokubeki 驚くべき
surroundings kankyô 環境
survive, to ikinobiru 生き延びる
suspect, to utagau 疑う
suspicion kengi 嫌疑
stubborn dankotoshita 断固とした
swallow, to nomikomu 飲み込む
sweat hakkan 発汗
sweat, to ase o kaku 汗をかく
sweep, to haku 掃く
sweet amai 甘い
sweet (dessert) dezâto デザート
sweet and sour amazuppai 甘酸っぱい
sweets (candy) ame 飴

S

ENGLISH–JAPANESE

sweetcorn suîtokôn スイートコーン
swim, to oyogu 泳ぐ
swimming costume, swimsuit mizugi 水着
swimming pool pûru プール
swing, to yuri ugokasu 揺り動かす
switch suicchi スイッチ
switch, to (change) kôkansuru 交換する
switch, to (clothes) kigaeru 着替える
switch on, to tsukeru 点ける
synthetic gôsei no 合成の

T

table tsukue 机, têburu テーブル
tablecloth têburukurosu テーブルクロス
tablemat têburumatto テーブルマット
tablets jôzai 錠剤
Tagalog tagarogu(jin) no タガログ（人）の
tail o 尾, shippo しっぽ
take, to (remove) motteiku 持っていく
take care of, to sewa o suru 世話をする
take off, to (clothes) nugu 脱ぐ（服）
talk, to hanasu 話す
talk about, to ~ni tsuite hanasu ～について話す
tall takai 高い
tame jûjun na 従順な
Taoism dôkyô 道教
tape, adhesive secchaku têpu 接着テープ
tape recording têpu no rokuon テープの録音
taste aji 味
taste, to (sample) shishoku o suru 試食をする
taste, to (salty, spicy, etc.) ajimi o suru 味見をする
tasty oishii おいしい
taxi takushî タクシー
tea cha 茶
teach, to oshieru 教える
teacher sensei 先生
team chîmu チーム
tear, to (rip) yaburu 破る
tears namida 涙
teenager shishunki no kodomo 思春期の子供（13～19歳）
teeshirt tyîshatsu ティーシャツ
teeth ha 歯
telephone denwa 電話
telephone number denwabangô 電話番号
television terebi テレビ
tell, to (a story) hanasu 話す
tell, to (let know) oshieru 教える
temperature ondo 温度
temple (ancient) koji 古寺
temple jiin 寺院, tera 寺
temporary ichijiteki na 一時的な
ten jû 十
ten thousand ichiman 一万
tendon ken 腱
tennis tenisu テニス
tens of (multiples of ten) nanjûbaimono 何十倍もの
tense kinchôshita 緊張した
terrible hidoi ひどい
test shiken 試験, tesuto テスト
test, to tamesu 試す
testicles kôgan 睾丸
than ~yori ～より
Thai tai(jin) no タイ（人）の
Thailand tai タイ
thank, to kanshasuru 感謝する
thank you arigatô ありがとう
that (introducing a quotation) ~to (iu) ～と（言う）

that person sono hito その人
that are あれ
that thing sore それ
theater (drama) gekijo 劇場
their, theirs karera no 彼らの
then sono go その後, sorekara それから
there soko ni そこに, soko de そこで
there is/are ~ga aru ～がある, ~ga iru ～がいる
therefore sono kekka その結果
these korera no これらの
they, them karera wa/o 彼らは/を
thick (of liquids) koi 濃い
thick (of things) atsui 厚い
thief dorobô 泥棒
thigh momo もも
thin (of liquids) usui 薄い（液体）
thin (of persons) yaseta やせた（人）
thing mono 物
think, to (have an opinion) omou 思う
think, to (ponder) kangaeru 考える
third daisan no 第三の
thirsty nodo no kawaita のどの渇いた
thirteen jûsan 十三
thirty sanjû 三十
this kono この
those arera あれら
though ~nimo kakawarazu ～にもかかわらず
thoughts shikô 思考
thousand sen 千
thread ito 糸
threaten, to kyôhakusuru 脅迫する
three san 三
throat nodo のど
through (past) ~o tôrinukete ～を通り抜けて
throw, to nageru 投げる
throw away/out, to suteru 捨てる
thunder kaminari 雷
Thursday mokuyôbi 木曜日
thus (so) shitagatte 従って
ticket (for entertainment) ken 券, chiketto チケット（娯楽）
ticket (for transport) kippu 切符（乗り物）
tidy sêtonsareta 整頓された
tidy up, to sêtonsuru 整頓する
tie (necktie) nekutai ネクタイ
tie, to musubu 結ぶ
tiger tora トラ
tight pittarishita ぴったりした, kitsui きつい
time jikan 時間
time: from time to time tokidoki 時々
times (multiplying) bai 倍
timetable jikokuhyô 時刻表
tiny totemo chîsa na とても小さな
tip (end) hashi 端
tip (gratuity) chippu チップ, kokorozuke 心付け
tired (sleepy) nemui 眠い
tired (worn out) tsukareta 疲れた
title (of book, film) daimei 題名（本、映画）
title (of person) katagaki 肩書き（人）
to (a person) ~e ～へ, ~no hô ni ～の方に（人）
to (a place) ~e ～へ, ~no hôkô ni ～の方向に（場所）
toasted aburareta あぶられた
today kyô 今日
toe tsumasaki つま先
tofu tôfu 豆腐
together tomo ni 共に, issho ni 一緒に
toilet tearai 手洗い, toire トイレ
tomato tomato トマト
tomorrow asu 明日

tongue shita 舌
tonight konban 今晩
too (also) ~mo mata ～もまた
too (excessive) amari ni~sugiru あまりに～過ぎる
too much ôsugiru 多過ぎる
tool dôgu 道具
tooth ha 歯
toothbrush haburashi 歯ブラシ
toothpaste hamigakiko 歯磨き粉
top ue 上
topic wadai 話題
torch (flashlight) kaichûdentô 懐中電灯
total gôkei (no) 合計（の）
touch, to fureru 触れる
tourist kankôkyaku 観光客
toward ~no hôe ～の方へ
toward, to ~e mukau ～へ向かう
towel taoru タオル
tower tô 塔
town machi 町
toy omocha おもちゃ
trade (business) shôbai 商売
trade (exchange) bôeki 貿易
tradition dentô 伝統
traditional dentôteki na 伝統的な
traffic kôtsû 交通
train densha 電車
train station eki 駅
training kunren 訓練
translate, to honyakusuru 翻訳する
travel, to ryokô o suru 旅行をする
traveler ryokôsha 旅行者
tray bon 盆
treat (something special) tanoshimi 楽しみ, gochisô ご馳走
treat, to (deal with) atsukau 扱う
treat, to (medically) chiryôsuru 治療する
tree ki 木
triangle sankaku 三角
tribe buzoku 部族
trip (journey) tabi 旅
troops guntai 軍隊
trouble konnan 困難
troublesome mendô na 面倒な
trousers zubon ズボン
truck torakku トラック
true hontô no 本当の
truly hontô ni 本当に
trust, to shinraisuru 信頼する
try, to doryokusuru 努力する
try on, to (clothes) shichakusuru 試着する
Tuesday kayôbi 火曜日
turn: to make a turn magaru 曲がる
turn around, to furikaeru 振りかえる
turn off, to kesu 消す
turn on, to tsukeru 点ける
turtle (land) rikugame 陸亀
turtle (sea) umigame 海ガメ
TV terebi テレビ
twelve jûni 十二
twenty nijû 二十
two ni 二
type (sort) shurui 種類
type, to taipusuru タイプする
typhoon taihû 台風
typical tenkeiteki na 典型的な

U

ugly migurushii 見苦しい
umbrella kasa 傘
uncle oji おじ
uncooked nama no 生の
under ~no shita ni ～の下に
undergo, to keikensuru 経験する
underpants pantsu パンツ
undershirt hadagi 肌着
understand, to rikaisuru 理解する
underwear shitagi 下着

undressed, to get fuku o nugu 服を脱ぐ
unemployed shitsugyôchû no 失業中の
unfortunately zannen nagara 残念ながら
unhappy fukô na 不幸な
United Kingdom eikoku 英国
United States amerika gasshûkoku アメリカ合衆国
university daigaku 大学
unless ~de nai kagiri ～でない限り
unlucky fuun na 不運な
unnecessary fuhitsuyô na 不必要な
unripe miseijuku no 未成熟の
until ~made ～まで
up, upward ue no hôe 上のほうへ
upset dôyôshita 動揺した
upside down sakasama 逆さま
upstairs jôkai e 上階へ
urban toshi no 都市の
urge, to (push for) shôdô o karitateru 衝動を駆り立てる
urgent kinkyû no 緊急の
urinate, to shôben o suru 小便をする
use, to tsukau 使う
used to (accustomed) nareteiru 慣れている
used to do something yoku ~shitamonoda よく～したものだ
useful yakudatsu 役立つ
useless mueki na 無益な
usual itsumo no いつもの
usually futsû wa 普通は
uterus shikyû 子宮
utensil dôgu 道具

V

vacation kyûka 休暇
vaccination yobôsesshu 予防接種
vagina chitsu 膣
vague aimai na あいまいな
valid yûkô na 有効な, datô na 妥当な
valley tani 谷
value (cost) kachi 価格
value (good) oneuchi お値打ち
value, to nebumi o suru 値踏みをする
vase kabin 花瓶
VCR bideo dekki ビデオデッキ
vegetable yasai 野菜
vehicle norimono 乗り物
verify tashikameru 確かめる
very (extremely) hijô ni 非常に
vest besuto ベスト, chokki チョッキ
via ~o tootte ～を通って
video cassette bideo kasetto ビデオカセット
video recorder bideo rekôdâ ビデオレコーダー
videotape, to rokugasuru 録画する
Vietnam betonamu ベトナム
Vietnamese betonamu(jin) no ベトナム（人）の
view (panorama) keshiki 景色
viewpoint mikata 見方
village mura 村
vinegar su 酢
visa biza ビザ, sashô 査証
visit taizai 滞在
visit: pay a visit to tazuneru 訪ねる
voice koe 声
voicemail rusubandenwa 留守番電話
volcano kazan 火山
vomit, to hakidasu 吐き出す
vote, to tôhyôsuru 投票する

W

wages chingin 賃金
wait for, to ~o motsu ～を待つ
waiter, waitress kyûji 給仕

W

ENGLISH–JAPANESE

wake someone up, to okosu 起こす
wake up, to mezameru 目覚める
Wales wêruzu ウェールズ
walk, to aruku 歩く
walking distance aruite ikeru kyori 歩いて行ける距離
wall kabe 壁
wallet saifu 財布
want, to ~ga hoshii ～が欲しい, ~shitai ～したい
war sensô 戦争
war: to start a war sensô o hajimeru 戦争を始める
warm atatakai 暖かい
warmth nukumori ぬくもり
warn, to kêkokusuru 警告する
warning kêkoku 警告
wash, to arau 洗う
wash the dishes, to shokki o arau 食器を洗う
watch (wristwatch) udedokei 腕時計
watch, to miru 見る
watch, to (show, movie) miru 観る
watch over, to (guard) miharu 見張る
water mizu 水
water buffalo suigyû 水牛
waterfall taki 滝
watermelon suika スイカ
wave (in sea) nami 波
wave, to furu 振る
wax wakkusu ワックス, rô ロウ
way (method) hôhô 方法
way: the way of ~suru hôhô ～する方法
way in iriguchi 入口
way out deguchi 出口
we, us (excludes the one addressed) watashitachi no/wa 私たちの/は
we, us (includes the one addressed) watashitachi wa/o 私たちは/を
weak yowai 弱い
wealthy yûfuku na 裕福な
weapon buki 武器
wear, to kiru 着る
weary tsukarekitta 疲れ切った
weather tenki 天気
weave, to oru 織る
weaving orimono 織り物
website webusaito ウェブサイト
wedding kekkonshiki 結婚式
Wednesday suiyôbi 水曜日
week shû 週
weekend shûmatsu 週末
weekly maishû no 毎週の
weep, to naku 泣く
weigh, to hakaru 量る
weigh out, to hakari wakeru 量り分ける
weight omosa 重さ
weight, to gain taijû ga fueru 体重が増える
weight, to lose taiju ga heru 体重が減る
welcome! yôkoso ようこそ
welcome to ~e yôkoso ～へようこそ
well (for water) ido 井戸
well (good) yoi 良い
well done! yoku dekimashita よくできました
well off (wealthy) yûfuku na 裕福な
well-behaved, well-mannered gyôgi no ii 行儀のいい
well-cooked, well-done yoku hi no tootta よく火の通った
Welsh wêruzu(jin) no ウェールズ（人）の
west nishi 西

westerner seiyôjin 西洋人
wet nureta 濡れた
what nani 何
what for nan no tame ni 何のために
what happened nani ga okitano 何が起きたの
what kind of donna どんな
what time nanji 何時
wheel sharin 車輪
when itsu いつ
when (at the time) ~suru toki ～する時
whenever itsudemo いつでも
where doko どこ
where to doko e どこへ
which dore どれ
while (during) ~no aida ni ～の間に
white shiro 白
who dare だれ
whole (all of) subete no 全ての
whole (to be complete) kanzen na 完全な
why naze なぜ
wicked warui 悪い
wide habahiroi 幅広い
width haba 幅
widow mibôjin 未亡人
will ~deshô ～でしょう
with ~to ～と
within reason dôri ni kanatteiru 道理にかなっている
without ~nashi ni ～なしに
witness mokugekisha 目撃者
witness, to mokugekisuru 目撃する
woman josei 女性
wonderful subarashii すばらしい
wood ki 木
wooden mokusei no 木製の
wool yômô 羊毛
word go 語, kotoba 言葉
work (occupation) shigoto 仕事
work, to shigoto o suru 仕事をする
work, to (function) kinôsuru 機能する
world sekai 世界
worn out (clothes, machine) tsukaifurushita 使い古した（服、機械）
worn out (tired) tsukarekitta 疲れ切った
worry, to shinpaisuru 心配する
worse yori warui より悪い
worship, to shinkôsuru 信仰する
worst mottomohidoi 最もひどい
worth, to be kachigaaru 価値がある
wound kega 怪我
wrap, to tsutsumu 包む
wrist tekubi 手首
write, to kaku 書く
writer sakka 作家
wrong (false) ayamatta 誤った
wrong (mistaken) machigatta 間違った
wrong (morally) warui 悪い（道徳的に）

Y

yawn, to akubisuru あくびする
year toshi 年
years old ~sai ～歳
yell, to sakebu 叫ぶ
yellow kîro 黄色
yes hai はい
yesterday kinô 昨日
yet: not yet mada~nai まだ～ない
you (familiar) anata あなた
you (female) anata あなた
you (male) kimi 君

Y

ENGLISH—JAPANESE

you're welcome dôitashimashite どういたしまして

young wakai 若い

younger brother otôto 弟

younger sister imôto 妹

youth (state of being young) wakasa 若さ

youth (young person) wakamono 若者

Z

zero zero 零

zoo dôbutsuen 動物園

zucchini zukkîni ズッキーニ